Process-Based Software Project Management

Other Auerbach Publications in Software Development, Software Engineering, and Project Management

Process-Based Software Project Management

F. Alan Goodman

CRC Press
Taylor & Francis Group
Boca Raton London New York

CRC Press is an imprint of the
Taylor & Francis Group, an **informa** business

AN AUERBACH BOOK

CRC Press
Taylor & Francis Group
6000 Broken Sound Parkway NW, Suite 300
Boca Raton, FL 33487-2742

First issued in paperback 2019

ISBN-13: 978-0-8493-7304-6 (hbk)
ISBN-13: 978-0-367-40359-1 (pbk)

Library of Congress Card Number 2005058918

Library of Congress Cataloging-in-Publication Data

Goodman, F. Alan.
    Process based software project management / F. Alan Goodman.
        p. cm.
    Includes bibliographical references and index.
    ISBN 0-8493-7304-2 (alk. paper)
    1. Computer software--Development--Management. I. Title.

QA76.76.D47G6534 2006
005.1'068--dc22
                                                          2005058918

Visit the Taylor & Francis Web site at
http://www.taylorandfrancis.com

and the CRC Press Web site at
http://www.crcpress.com

Dedication

I dedicate this book to my wife Corinne,
whose Parkinson's Disease has robbed her
of any shared joy that she would have had
in my writing accomplishments.

Contents

List of Figures

List of Tables

About the Author

F. Alan Goodman has over 20 years' experience in the software process field. He is now an independent process consultant in the San Diego area. Al holds a MScEE degree from the University of California (Santa Barbara). His extensive background covers both commercial and DoD contracting software engineering environments. Al has had all possible software engineering-related roles throughout his career in both management and nonmanagement positions.

Al has been the past president of the San Diego chapter of the Society for Software Quality (SSQ) for two years. He has taught computer-related courseware at West Coast University and National University in San Diego at both the undergraduate and graduate levels. Al has also been a presenter at the Software Engineering Group (SEPG), Society for Software Quality (SSQ), San Diego Computer Society, and the San Diego Project Management Institute (PMI). He has California teaching credentials for engineering topics at the college level. He is currently pursuing being an adjunct professor at the University of California at San Diego (UCSD) Extension. He will teach "Process-Based Software Project Management" where he will apply his process approach to the real world of software project management.

For more information on the author, please see www.theprocessguy. com.

Preface

After writing "Defining and Deploying Software Processes" [1], it struck me that the biggest beneficiary of this process architectural model approach was the software project manager. I kept uncovering values for any software project manager who used this underlying process framework model. I will admit that many of my anecdotal stories are a direct result of seeing a range of Software Project Management (SPM) expertise that covered the entire spectrum of really bad to really good. I can also relate some of my own experiences as a new SPM trying to follow company rules for getting the job done. I must also admit that the part of being a software project manager that I really hated was dealing with the politics of the job. I concluded that I was just too darn honest for spinning project progress beyond the realm of reality into a fantasy world. I have also run into my share of SPMs who act like some neurosurgeons (i.e., above "normal" people) and are not about to have anyone tell them that a right process approach helps them significantly. I suspect these "I know it all — don't bother me" folks will not read this book at all. For those of you who want a better way of doing your job, this book's for you.

I'm predominately a "process guy" who has had almost every role possible within a software engineering environment. This makes me a generalist due to my broad background in many facets of development and project management. My background has also included being a university adjunct professor teaching computer topics at both the undergraduate and graduate levels. I mention this because I'm going to come at software project management from a "process guy" point of view.

What you will discover as you go through this book is not only a tight coupling of processes with the SPM but also a tight coupling with:

- Software engineering
- Software configuration management
- Software quality assurance
- Accounting
- Earned value people
- Metrics people

I have purposely written in a style that I hope is easily read by a range of people from software leads through to company executives. I have written this book as if I were talking to you. I have made a conscious effort to not make this an "academia" book. My main objective is to leave the reader with a really good understanding of where I'm coming from and to show how a tight coupling to this process model approach will really turn the act of managing software projects on its end for many of you. I hope to really change your mind about many aspects of SPM.

I am consciously aware that process is only good if it supports the organization. I have also run into fellow "process people" who have lost sight of this fact. Some companies have established a process bureaucracy for the sake of process. This type of company also has the "document everything that moves" kind of attitude. People who know me know that I am not in favor of papering the walls with processes. I believe in the motto "Be sensible about process." Not all things need to be documented. If I have learned anything as a "process guy," it's that people will follow and embrace processes if they are easy and make sense to them. If you try to ram processes down people's throats, the pushback will be unbelievable!

Anyway ... enjoy!

References

[1] "Defining and Deploying Software Processes" by F. Alan Goodman, Auerbach Publishers ISBN #0-8493-9845-2
[2] "Business Development Process" chart by Shipley Associates, 653 North main Street, P.O. Box 970, Farmington, UT 84025-0970 Tel: 801-451-2323

Introduction

There have been many books written about software project management (SPM). These books have mostly concentrated on:

- Software project management setup
- Software project management planning aspects
- Software project management tracking aspects
- Earned value
- Software project management customer interface elements
- Software project management project people management aspects
- Subcontractor selection related to software project management
- Subcontractor execution management related to software project management
- Risk management related to software project management
- Requirements management related to software project management
- Software project management closedown

Many consider SPM as primarily creating and managing project schedules along with some people skills. My book does <u>not</u> deal with people aspects of performing SPM. My book does <u>not</u> deal with risk management aspects of SPM. I do <u>not</u> deal with budgeting (cost accounts, contract budget baseline) except that I do describe a very different way of creating a WBS to support planning packages and work packages. The book's focus is on the process architecture role (or process underpinnings) in performing successful SPM. The process connection to software project management is not readily understood by traditional methods of software project management. Once you understand this process connection, you will realize that SPM can be accomplished totally in tune with your developmental processes. This process connection to SPM will automatically align SPM with all your ongoing software process improvements. These seemingly dissimilar worlds should be tightly coupled for incredible benefits but unfortunately are not embraced by many companies.

Most books have not addressed the important role that integrated process architecture performs in doing software project management. Many books look at software project management as a pipelined (and a separate) role that "sits on" whatever you have out there for your developmental processes. This process separation does just that — separates the SPM basis (schedule management primarily) from the development basis (software processes). This separation can lead to disastrous results.

If you subscribe to the notion that a major aspect of SPM is primarily involved with schedule creation and management, then the schedule tasks are really important for that SPM effort. We'll take a look at these schedule tasks.

Planning schedule tasks come from different sources:

- Software management/leads based on their proposed developmental approach
- Governmental/industry standards related to phases/deliverables
- Target project requirements for builds/capabilities
- Project SPM requirements for technical and management interchanges/reviews
- Internal company milestones/quality gates

Subsequent planning schedule tasks come from these different sources:

- Software management/leads based on increasing visibility from design
- Software management/leads based on integration planning
- Customer requirements changes affecting schedule tasking
- Software management/leads based on rework

These are the schedule tasks that get tracked during the course of any project. Because of the different sources of schedule tasks, it is highly probable that not all these schedule task contributors are on the same page for schedule task descriptions or task ordering. This is

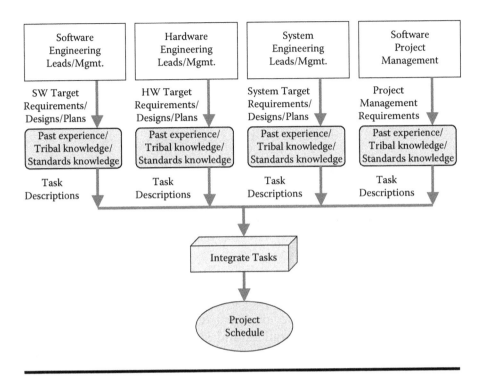

Figure 0.1   Immature company project scheduling.

particularly true for process-immature organizations where task descriptions and task ordering are *ad hoc* from each source. This is depicted graphically in Figure 0.1.

What you end up with are schedules that:

- Have different levels of detail
- Have a mix-and-match of verb-based task descriptions and noun-based task descriptions
- Have inconsistent descriptions across leads
- Have inconsistent implied task actions across leads
- Have inconsistent task ordering and connections
- Have no schedule connection to process architecture

If you recognize this scenario, you probably have the situation as portrayed in Figure 0.2.

These schedule tasks may be mostly divorced from your process architecture as practiced by your software developers. From a software project management perspective, if you get your schedule tasks done correctly, you should be able to plan and track project progress —

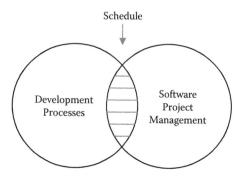

Schedule

Development
Processes

Software
Project
Management

Figure 0.2 Immature company Venn diagram.

right? The developers however, may be operating on a nonschedule basis (and usually are). If your process basis is not totally aligned with schedule tasking, the software project manager may be managing those tasks in a total void with development reality. I have personally seen this SPM/development separation, and it's not pretty.

When you align the software process world with the software project management schedule world, you align development with SPM by inserting a repeatable process filter to schedule task descriptions and ordering from your engineering organizations. This process filter applies a common, repeatable approach to tasking regardless of the source. This is shown graphically in Figure 0.3. When I talk about a process filter, I am talking about a process framework architecture that minimally separates "what you want done" from "how you are to do it" *and* has a 1:1 relationship of "what" process elements to generic tasks as seen on a schedule. I describe such process framework architecture in my previous book [1] and reinforce that description in this book. With this process approach, the SPM schedule tasks are merely instances of process "what you have to do" activity elements from the process world. Improvements in process content, deliverables, and ordering are picked up by SPM almost in real time. Process "what" element changes now have a 2-for-1 effect for both software project development and software project management. Process improvements show up during software development and are reflected by the SPM at the same time. This tight connection is a powerful force for a quality SPM effort.

If you have this process basis and apply this process filtering to develop schedule tasking, you have the situation as portrayed in Figure 0.4.

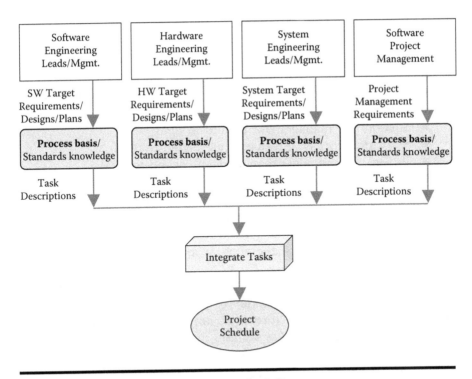

Figure 0.3   Mature company project scheduling.

Figure 0.4   Mature company Venn diagram.

If you're shaking your head at this point and wondering why this makes SPM so darn effective, stay tuned. I will show you that this strong process connection to SPM is extremely powerful for:

■ Software proposals
■ Software project management set up

- Software project estimation
- Software project planning
- Software project tracking
- Software project earned value calculations
- Software project planning package management to work packages
- Software project schedule rework management
- Subcontract management related to SPM
- Software process improvements related to SPM
- Project requirements management related to SPM
- Software quality related to SPM
- Software project management repeatability
- Software configuration management related to SPM
- Life cycle management related to SPM
- Software project management closedown

I will also show you what kinds of things need to be institutionalized to really support all this. I hope to demonstrate to you why your process framework architecture is so important for software project management. You can do SPM without that tight process coupling, but why would you? The bottom line for any SPM effort is to effectively plan and track progress. If the representation for progress (the project schedule) is <u>identical</u> to the development tasking *via* process, there is no separation and no misunderstandings between your engineering areas and SPM. Everyone is on the same page.

This book is broken into the following sections:

- Section I: Essence of Software Project Management. This sets the foundation for the book from a 40,000-foot view of SPM.
- Section II: Process Framework Architecture. This section describes the process approach that makes SPM so different than traditional approaches. It concentrates on those aspects of the process framework model pertinent to SPM and the SPM partners.
- Section III: Institutionalization Considerations. This section calls out those things that really need to be firmly embedded in your company culture to fully support SPM
- Section IV: Pre-execution Segment. This section is the first section that applies information from the first three sections to the front-end segment of any project life cycle.
- Section V: Execution Segment. This section applies information from the first three sections to the execution portion of any project life cycle.

I will provide a lot of examples throughout this book as I cover various aspect of SPM and show you why the process approach is so critical to SPM success. I'm a great believer in pictures reinforcing words. I hope to change your views about the role of process as it relates to SPM. Try to clear your mind of how you have done software project management in the past and allow me to offer you a far better way of performing this vital role.

I hope to show the readers that there are huge differences in this process-based software project management over traditional SPM. Traditional SPM assumes the role of trying to manage and control a bunch of software engineers in executing the project roadmap via a project schedule. This places the SPM as the sole lightning rod for attacks if things don't proceed as expected. In my method, key <u>engineering</u> personnel actually are responsible for identifying the schedule tasks and determine the ordering of those tasks on a project schedule — all based on process. I have absolutely removed the "us versus them" syndrome in software project management. Engineering, along with software configuration management, software quality, accounting, metrics personnel, and earned value personnel become true role partners with the SPM. This role division is very similar to a surgical team where different disciplines are involved for success, but there still is a chief surgeon who's running the show. The SPM is that chief surgeon. As you read through this book, this will become apparent to you.

ESSENCE OF SOFTWARE PROJECT MANAGEMENT

1

Chapter 1

The Software Project Management Big Picture

Introduction

Before getting into why the process of architectural underpinning is so vital for successful software project management (SPM), it is important to set the stage for the kinds of activities required to manage a software project. I used the word "successful" because you can certainly achieve varying levels of success that range from abominable to excellent. I have had personal experience of dealing with one SPM who could have easily run a death camp in a different era with no problem at all. The friction, shouting, and table thumping were some things that nobody looked forward to on a daily basis as a way to run a project. You can also achieve some level of success at SPM by pure brute force along with constant care and feeding of this SPM "beast." If you are (or know of) a software project manager who can't take a day off in case all hell breaks loose on your project, you will really need this book. I hope to show you that I can significantly reduce the SPM care and feeding aspect with this described, layered, and selectable process framework architecture as an SPM foundation.

I always like to start off with "the big picture." This provides the basis for all the elaborated topics that will be discussed. If you look at SPM from the 40,000-ft level, you could certainly see the SPM efforts involved within two major "buckets" of efforts:

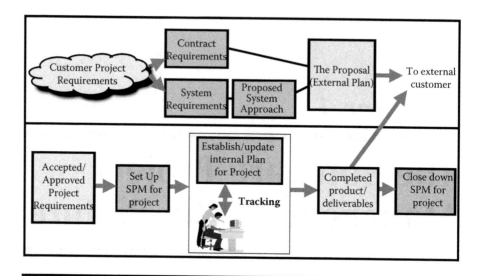

Figure 1.1   The SPM big picture for contractors.

- Project pre-execution efforts
- Project execution efforts

Having spent half of my career in the commercial world and the other half in the defense-contracting world, I can tell you that they are driven by very different needs. This 40,000-ft view is significantly different in the pre-execution part of the life cycle, culminating in a proposal submission. The execution part of the life cycle is, for all intents and purposes, very similar. I say "very similar" because government contractors are still in the documentation business a lot (imposed by the government), whereas commercial companies produce documentation only when needed. Another variant is the definition of "customer." Government contractors really have an external customer, whereas many commercial companies are very driven by internal customers (usually the marketing folks). That's the big difference at execution time. These are shown in Figure 1.1 and Figure 1.2, respectively.

I know that there are some out there who are saying, "Wait a minute — SPM is only involved once you start executing the project!" The reality is that SPM functions are involved in two stages. I have personally seen the scenario in which a proposal-type software project manager gets involved at pre-execution time, whereas a different software project manager performs at execution time. I can tell you from my experience that commitments can be made to the customer

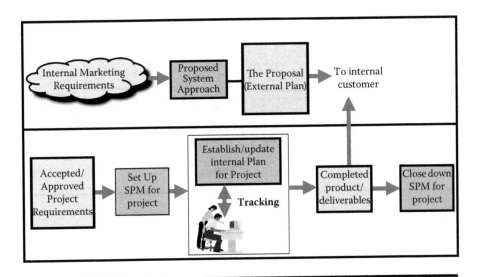

Figure 1.2   The SPM big picture for commercial companies.

at proposal time that any execution-time SPM would choke on. Proposal-time software project managers can commit to anything because they don't have to do the actual work. In fact, many times, this upfront software project manager can promise anything to get a "win." This mentality is especially prevalent in the government-contracting world. With a solid process/schedule/estimation connection, the probability of this separation gets decreased significantly (or eliminated) — even if two different individuals are involved. In an ideal world, the person who will be managing the execution work should be the same person who made those important commitments to the customer.

Pre-execution Efforts for Government Contractors

In the government-contracting world, you get customer requirements (or what I call "raw" customer requirements) given to you via a request for proposal (RFP) or request for quotation (RFQ). These requirements tend to be very disciplined with requirements clearly identified and with each requirement having a "shall." I mention the term "tend to be" because incoming requirements are quite often not normalized (the act of having discrete requirements) and clarified (semantic elaborations for ambiguous requirements). In addition to target-system requirements, the government also requires a whole host of contract requirements that are to show up throughout the development life

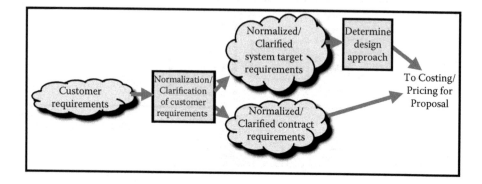

Figure 1.3   Contractor requirements definition flow.

cycle. The requirements definition story for contractor requirements is shown in Figure 1.3.

This figure shows that all requirements are separated into two "buckets:"

■ Target-system requirements
■ Nontarget-system requirements (i.e., contract requirements)

Even though contract requirements tend to be OK as is, there are many times when the incoming requirements are not normalized or clarified and still need that level of attention. Contract requirements are usually very clear and need only to be accounted for by the software project manager. These contract requirements deal with:

■ Major reviews, including the when-and-where aspects
■ Interface meetings, including meeting cycles, etc.
■ Deliverables, including how many and when
■ Status-reporting meetings

In addition to various reviews and meetings, the government identifies the set of deliverables (called contract data requirements list [CDRL]) by name, along with when they are to be produced and how many versions of each are needed. For many years, the government even went as far as identifying the exact format and contents needed for each deliverable by way of data item descriptions (DIDs). These formats tend to be more "contractor determined" today. All need to be cost estimated, be priced, and to show up on your external plan that goes back to the customer.

It has been my experience that system requirements always need to be normalized and at least partially clarified prior to doing any kind of design-approach determination. System requirements are usually voluminous but generally clear as to what is a requirement and what is not. It is these requirements that need a level of understanding and clarity to even come up with a proposed system approach. Here's the rub — you need to do enough requirements analysis and design to do a proposal but not enough to do the real work on your own dime! At this point, you're not paid for anything. You may not even get the contract! Having said that, it should be obvious to the reader that you want to reuse as much as possible from your proposal effort to get a head start at execution time. I have worked at a few companies where the attitude has been, "Well, that's that for proposals, and now we'll do the real thing at execution time!" In other words, the proposal effort can be considered fiction for the win only. It has nothing to do with what we really want to do! Both paths go on to costing and pricing as part of the estimating effort after design has been finalized.

At this point, there may be readers out there who are asking questions such as, "What is normalization?" and "What has this got to do with SPM?" *Normalization* is the act of decomposing multiple requirements embedded in a single English sentence into separate and discrete requirements. Requirements can get overlooked when they are not pulled out as discrete requirements. I'll provide an example in Figure 1.4 as to why project managers should be concerned about doing this. Although engineering performs requirements management activities, the impact on SPM can be huge if they are not done.

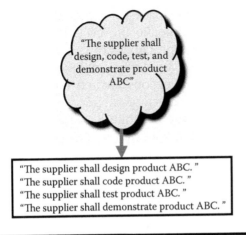

Figure 1.4 Requirements normalization example.

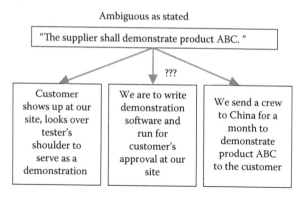

Figure 1.5   Requirements clarification example.

This example is taken from one company I worked for where normalization was not done. Omitting this step cost this company a small fortune. The original customer requirement was shown as a single English sentence, but it actually represented four requirements. In the real-world case, the last requirement about demonstrating was completely overlooked. That was a real "gotcha" for this company and the project manager. Only when you decompose incoming English sentences into discrete requirements (i.e., the act of normalizing) do you really know what you have without losing anything.

When you look at the normalized requirement in this example, it cries out to be clarified because its meaning is totally ambiguous. In Figure 1.5, I show graphically what kinds of thinking go into clarifying this ambiguous requirement example.

Something I learned a long time ago is that if you don't clarify, your customers will come back on you with their intent — usually way later in the developmental life cycle. Without clarification, true customer intentions were probably not factored into your efforts. It is in your own best interest to clarify ambiguous requirements — even in a vacuum. When clarifications are fed back to the customer, it is much better to adjust contract costs, prices, and durations on expectation differences than when nothing is done. In this real-world company, the last clarification was closer to what the customer expected than the first one. The cost and time differential was enormous. The company "ate it" with this oversight. As a "process guy," I suggested a customer meeting after a requirements pass-through for normalization and clarification to increase the "yes's" and decrease the "but's" related to requirements. The management of that company thought I was completely out of my mind. I just loved the reason for not doing this —

"We've never done that before!" It was my opinion that this would have been the best-attended meeting they'd ever have involving their customer, and that it would clear up any and all misunderstandings up front before effort occurs. This same company had customers in house at test time (close to the end of the life cycle), asking questions such as, "What the h@#& is this?", etc. Test time is not the right time to have surprises over contract expectations! The software project manager became the lightning rod for criticism and fault over this. I will show you that all this can be totally avoided with a process-based approach to SPM.

With system requirements normalized and partially clarified, we can now look at design approaches culminating in a proposed design. For design approach analysis, it is not my intent to endorse any specific technique, but I have personally used a Stuart-Pugh-type method very effectively for arriving at a winning proposal design. I mention this because you want to retain design alternatives, trade-offs, and design decisions made at proposal time as an input at execution time. Very often, the group making the proposal may not be the same players at execution time later on. The execution design team had better have really good insight into why the proposed design was selected and why other designs were not! No matter how you go about that, you should have a very firm and unambiguous foundation on which to base any proposed design.

As part of the proposed design approach, you need to determine if there are derived requirements. Logically, deriving requirements comes after proposal design, because you have better visibility on the proposed design direction. In my process model, I recommend a high-level step in the "determine design approach" activity specifically to make sure that deriving requirements are not overlooked. There's a lot of misinformation out there about derived requirements. Derived requirements occur mostly as a result of your domain knowledge that the customer does not have. Let's look at a roofing example. If you had to reroof your house, you would look over a variety of roofing materials presented by your roofing contractor. If you selected a reinforced-concrete roofing material versus a lighter-weight composition roof, there is a derived requirement that the roof be strengthened to support that extra weight. The contractor knows this and should include this additional effort in the estimate of costs and time that would not have shown up on a lighter-weight roofing selection. You only wanted that particular type of roof. The contractor-added derived requirement didn't come from you. Again, there may be software project

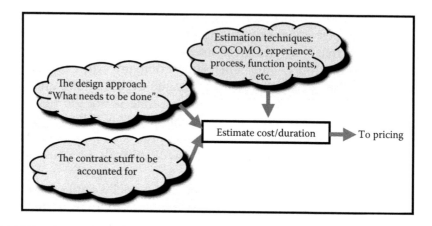

Figure 1.6   Estimation model story for costs.

managers reading this that would take exception to the notion that deriving requirements is important to them. After all, doesn't engineering do this? Similar to other factors, if whole sections of work are not factored in for cost and effort, guess who will take the hit for this? It's the project manager.

At this point, we enter the wonderful world of estimations based on a proposed design approach plus all the other contractual stuff needed, and we come up with, among other items:

- Estimated cost
- Estimated durations
- Estimated manpower loading

This top-level view is given in Figure 1.6.

Here's another instance where system aspects and nonsystem aspects are treated very differently. There are several established estimation techniques for software. Methods such as source lines of code (SLOC) estimations have been around for years. Function point analysis is another — especially for software applications. Programs such as COCOMO, etc., can be used as well. Then you have my all-time favorite method of "I know what I'm doing — it will take xxx months at a cost of $yyy," with no backing whatsoever. Later in this book, I will show you a process-based estimation technique that can supplement whatever approaches you currently use. This technique will serve as a validation (or not) of how you're currently doing business. I will also show you that you can reuse the whole front end of my technique for your execution-time schedule — a veritable two-for-one sale.

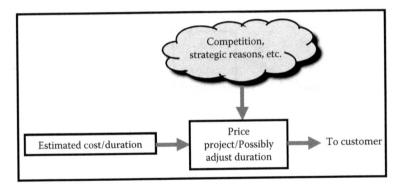

Figure 1.7 Pricing top-level story.

Once we have a cost understanding of the tasks and their magnitude, we enter the pricing world. This can be graphically shown, as in Figure 1.7.

As I stated earlier, the customer pricing on this project may not be higher than the cost! There may be either strategic or competitive reasons for having a low price. The margins here may be low or negative. This is one area that I know some software project managers get confused about. Costs are internal estimates to do the work, whereas the price is the external bid to the customer. Project managers need to track costs, not price! Your pricing the project lower than the estimated costs should not be a reason for beating up engineering if they exceed the price boundary.

In both the big-picture figures, you'll notice that I use the term "external plan" as something different from an "internal plan." The external plan is merely your best estimate of what it will take to do the work at a certain price and duration. Estimates can range from a seat-of-the-pants estimate to a highly structured and disciplined approach to estimates. At one place I worked, the estimates were based on round numbers and whether they could stick on the wall for a few minutes! It is the external plan that goes to the customer. The internal plan is the one that you actually use to track project progress. If you ever want to see some ugly SPM and engineering fights, try using the external plan to track progress! Some software project managers confuse these plans. Keep in mind that the external plan is your best guess sent to the customer. Some managers also confuse cost versus price as well, which can also cause massive fights. The price is something that is of interest to your customer, whereas the cost is your internal estimate to finish the work. There are companies out there that do this erroneously.

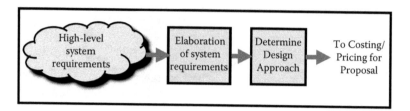

Figure 1.8 Commercial requirements definition flow.

In the contracting environment, the external plan is a huge document, the format of which is dictated by the government. Quite often, the external plan is so large that it's in multiple volumes. Preparation of this work product is a major effort. This document has all the pretty print graphics, foldouts, and glossies for a "wow" marketing document.

Pre-execution Efforts for Commercial Companies

Unlike the government-contracting world, you may get requirements from your internal marketing people to stay competitive. The requirements definition story for commercial companies is shown in Figure 1.8.

These requirements may be of such high level that you absolutely have to define what they mean. I once worked for a large cellular telecommunications company in which one such requirement was, "We need roaming." That was the requirement! I would certainly not call this disciplined. You may never see a "shall" in this environment. At this point, the incoming "requirement" is up in the stratosphere. In this commercial world, it falls on the shoulders of systems engineering to create a set of real requirements based on the statement "We need roaming." The reader may notice that I did not include normalization and clarification in this flow. This omission was done on purpose. Hopefully, your own internal people generate normalized and clarified requirements out of the gate when doing any kind of elaboration of requirements. I would also hope that they introduce any needed derived requirements. If they don't, then provide requirements training for your staff as a corrective action measure. All this action goes on in the box labeled "Elaboration of System Requirements." After getting some real-looking (normalized, clarified, and derived) requirements, you can proceed further with determining the design approach.

Unlike the government-contracting world, you don't get contract requirements — you just get target-system requirements. All nonsystem tasks or events usually come from the company's life-cycle way of doing business and not from the outside. Also, documents tend to be minimal and are only produced when there's some value to the organization. Commercial companies are not going to spend time and effort creating fancy documents for their own consumption. It's just not going to happen. The external plan in this environment is quite often very informal (because it's essentially going back to marketing), covering, among other considerations:

- Can we do it?
- When we can produce?
- What might suffer?

For commercial companies, the system analysis at proposal time tends to be a whole lot less rigorous than the government-contracting world and is also much faster. Commercial companies really want a general feel for impact on continuing development to insert this new marketing requirement. The concept of "my dime" (proposal time) versus "your dime" (execution time) is nonexistent because, quite often, there is no external customer. Unfortunately, many commercial companies do not do a good job of retaining design decisions, trade-offs, etc., at proposal time because the normal working pace is hectic. I have also seen the effects of not doing this properly, especially when you have a large and dynamic workforce. They could spend a lot of time at execution time (when it counts for time to market) trying to figure out why this design was called out? Why not that design, etc.? The proverb "penny wise and pound foolish" comes to mind here.

Both environments need to cost out the estimated effort. Typically, in the commercial world, pricing is wholly contained in the marketing world and is totally separated from the SPM/development world. Pricing is totally divorced from the development environment.

Even though you might not have an external customer, I still use the term "external plan" as something different from an "internal plan." The external plan, even if it's going to marketing, is merely your best estimate of what it will take to do the work and when it can be done. With one of my employers, that external plan was a PowerPoint slide.

Execution Efforts for Both

You'll notice that Figure 1.1 and Figure 1.2 look the same for the execution segment. These representations are essentially true, with the following caveats:

Government-contracting execution:

- Acceptance/approval may never happen! The fact that you submitted a proposal does not ensure that you'll get to execute that project! Unless this is a sole-source type of contract, the execution segment may not exist.
- Acceptance/approval is a very formal process via the contracts department.
- Time delay between an external plan submission and any "go-ahead" could take months. The government goes through a vetting of all submissions that could include site visits, capability audits, and a scoring process against all submitters.

Commercial company execution:

- Acceptance/approval is almost certainly a slam-dunk because marketing wants additional capabilities and features. They have a vested interest to provide that go-ahead.
- Acceptance/approval is very informal. I've seen this done verbally and via e-mail. No contracts department involvement at all.
- Time delay between an external plan submission and any go-ahead is extremely short. It is effectively a sole-source situation.

No matter what, you do need some type of project setup at the beginning of the execution segment. This involves various things such as setting up development repositories, charge numbers, process basis, etc. I will talk a lot more about this later.

The big event during the execution segment is project planning and tracking. This is the bulk of any execution segment for time and effort. Both government contractors and commercial companies need to do planning and tracking. The centerpiece of project planning and tracking is the project schedule. I devote Chapter 2 to this aspect of the execution segment because it is a key component of this process-based SPM approach. As you read on, I will show you why the schedule is by far the most important work product you have in managing any software project. In my approach, every schedule task has a direct connection to the process world for consistency, repeatability, earned value, quality gates, metrics data collection, and software configuration management (SCM) control hooks. Most companies do not have this process–schedule task connection and suffer a lot because of it. I will show you why this is crucial to SPM and why you really need to think hard about incorporating this process approach [1] into your company for effective SPM. I am passionate about this process approach that supports SPM and hope to get the readers excited about this, too! I will bring up this topic throughout this book, showing many reasons why there are huge benefits in adopting this method.

From this 40,000-ft level, we deliver the product and deliverables to the customer. I remind the reader again that the customer can be external or internal.

At the execution end, you have some kind of project "closedown." Commercial companies tend to be more informal and shorter than government contractors. Closedown happens anyway. This involves various things such as closing down development repositories, charge numbers, etc. It's a good idea to have a postmortem to look back at what was done right and what could be done differently. I will also talk a lot more about this in Chapter 16.

Chapter 2

Planning and Tracking: The Big Picture

Introduction

In Chapter 1, a box is shown (Figure 1.1 and Figure 1.2) for planning and tracking in both the government-contracting world and the commercial world of software project management (SPM). That is the whole game as far as any software project manager is concerned. It is for this reason that I am dealing with this "big-picture view" separately in this chapter.

This big-picture view tends to be the traditional way of looking at planning and tracking. In reality, you have two plans:

- Proposal-time plan (external plan) for project estimation cost, price, and duration, primarily done for the software project customer. This effort can range from a fully delivered plan (for the government contractor) to a roll-up summary for end price, period of performance, or end date (for commercial companies) based on the estimation plan. This estimation, by definition, has to include the entire cradle-to-grave story for the project. I want to point out again that this is your best guess and may have nothing to do with system reality at execution time. You may have estimated five subsystems at proposal time only to find out later that you actually have six subsystems at execution time!

- Execution-time plan (internal plan) that is primarily used for planning/tracking purposes to manage progress on the project. This plan, by definition, has to reflect reality at execution time. That means that it has to be incremental. It can't start out as a cradle-to-grave story. You simply don't know everything up front. Only by executing top-level design tasks do you even know the system and subsystem piece/part story. Only by following the integration plan do you know the proper implementation ordering and integration ordering of those pieces/parts.

Proposal-Time Planning

You plan a project at a very rough level if you have a proposal phase in your project's life cycle. Most government-contracting companies need to respond to a government proposal with that initial planning story. Many commercial companies need to respond to competitive challenges quickly, and this drives their initial plan. It is this plan that becomes the basis for an initial understanding on what needs to be done at execution time and for how much. It always amazes me when I see plans produced early as part of the bid process being totally ignored when the job is to be executed. It's similar to a "that was then" and "this is now" kind of attitude.

For any external plan submitted to the (usually government) customer, you lay all this out at the summary level merely because it is derived as a result of estimation. Many commercial enterprises have no such thing as a deliverable external schedule and merely give an end date for completion along with a cost. These same companies really do have a "hip pocket" external plan that supports that end date. Any external plan is characterized by the following:

- Noun-based phases, deliverables, or reviews
- Summary based (no lower-level tasking)
- Giving a top-level view

Figure 2.1 shows the summary aspect of an external schedule.

Believe it or not, this estimation planning data can come from thin air (10,000 hr seems a really nice round number ...), or it can come from a solid estimation basis. If you do project planning based on round numbers, you deserve bad SPM. If you have a mature organization and have a database of prior actuals based on similar projects,

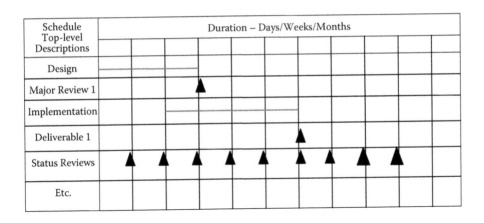

Figure 2.1   General aspects of an external schedule.

you will have a really good idea of what this new effort will entail. Past estimations can provide enough data to present to a customer to give that feel for length and cost of any described effort.

A good process repository develops better and better estimation data exactly for this cause. This is an area where you can get into source lines of code (SLOC) estimates, function points, past experience, etc. I will leave it to the reader to deduce how this planning data gets derived. Generally, two approaches and consolidation are the best validation approach to this.

I hope to show you that the process framework architecture itself can do wonders in this area to get better (and more accurate) estimation data that can be used for external planning. I still advocate a second estimation approach to validate the resultant data. I want to reiterate that this estimation planning data is just that — it only provides overall guidance. It will not serve as an execution piece/part roadmap even though some software project managers try to do this. Throughout my government-contracting days, I found that this double usage seemed to be the norm, which consequently caused all kinds of problems, both internally and externally. I will show you that by using the process basis for the initial external planning, you can come close to approximating the whole thing to start your execution! The customer "plan" and the developer "plan" come from the same basis — not separate ones.

The biggest problem that software project managers may have at execution time is that the proposal-time planning may be way off the mark for budget, time, and resources. All of which factor into the pricing of this project. Remember, you can't be profitable in your pricing if you don't have a good handle on your costs. Companies that don't pay attention to this tend to go out of business. Your customer needs to get the impression that you know what you're doing. You need proper costing for resource management and personnel availability. You need something as a roadmap. Human resources need this to staff your project. You don't know where you are if you don't have a map. This should be the "map." For government contractors, this external project planning is usually a required deliverable. Commercial companies need to do external project planning properly to be profitable and stay in business.

This is where the cost account management (CAM) system can really bite you. You have to break down all estimated work into cost accounts. Typically this breakdown is by logical functional areas. For example, if you were building a house, cost accounts (a layer of your work breakdown structure) might include, among others, the following:

- Foundation
- Framing
- Plumbing
- Electrical
- Drywall

Within each cost account, you'd have a further breakdown that is reflected in the work breakdown structure (WBS). Physically, these areas of work tend to be done by different people with different skills. Each of these areas would ultimately have a cost account manager, a budget, a period of performance, and resource data. Complications arise because the budget is not a monolithic number, but is a distributed budget over a calendar that can be further grouped into fiscal year budgets. The budgeting part of this is probably a book unto itself. I will just skim over this topic — only relating parts of this to the presented process-based SPM approach.

The unfortunate thing that happens is that any cost account manager (at execution time) is stuck with proposal-time planning packages. These planning packages really reflect future work within a cost account that has not yet become work packages. Planning packages have firm budgets, estimated start and end dates, and a statement of work. Planning packages are usually around six months in duration. Here's the rub — any deviation from a planning package to a work package (at execution time) carries a heavy burden filling out deviation and revision requests or reports and "taking the gas pipe" over those variances. The approach I'll describe can make things considerably easier if you use the process as a basis for estimation that, in turn, becomes the basis for planning packages. I will revisit this topic later when I show you how you can effectively use this process-based SPM for proposal or pre-execution estimations and also reuse quite of lot of that work for project execution to improve the integrity of your planning packages.

At execution time, I advocate having a just-in-time schedule based on your process activity diagrams (PADs; more on that later) to really reflect reality for the developer, software project manager, software configuration manager, and quality engineers alike.

The Software Project Schedule

The software project manager's big "plan" is really the software project schedule. That's the single-most important work product there is in managing projects. It is also the one item that regularly "misses the mark" as an indicator of "done" and is the major focus of disgruntlement for all levels of management when tasks are not met. For many companies, the schedule is viewed as "that thing the software project manager deals with" — not as an integrated work product on which workers and management are all focused. I have personally seen cases in which software leads had their schedules and the software project manager had his or her own schedule. These same leads would have updated the "other schedule" to satisfy the software project manager whether it reflects reality or not. It's no wonder we get into trouble managing software projects when this type of stuff is going on. The probability that these two schedules are synchronized is slim to zero. My approach treats the SPM schedule as the one-and-only schedule for planning and tracking, using a process-basis approach to SPM.

I have always been amazed at what some people think a project plan is. The initial schedule by itself is a plan. As I have stated before, this is the major artifact for any software project manager. Some other things are derived from that schedule plan that do need to be described elsewhere. Let's look at what the schedule itself can provide; it includes the following:

- Project start and finish
- Project duration
- Tasks
- Task ordering

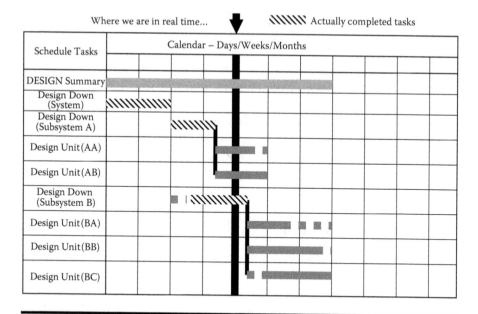

Figure 2.2 Typical internal planning/tracking schedule.

- Tasking responsibilities
- Project life cycle developmental approach
- Major revisions and reviews
- Manpower loading
- Level of effort (LOE) activities
- Deliverables

Some readers may take exception to the emphasis on the schedule itself and feel that there are other important artifacts used in SPM, such as:

- Data management spreadsheets for deliverable controls
- Project metrics and charts
- Various accounting spreadsheets related to budgets, costs, and estimated time to complete projects, earned value, etc.
- Monthly status reports, etc.

All these are secondary to the software project schedule. The schedule drives a lot of these ancillary artifacts and, therefore, I will not address these secondary work products. If the schedule gets done right, other things will follow suit.

If you could step back and look at a schedule, you can see that it is merely a representation of the complete workflow necessary to get from the beginning to the end of any project. I am a big proponent of the idea that an execution-time planning schedule should never have anything on it that does not reflect reality. I don't want to see planning package representations superimposed on my schedule, because they don't reflect reality. Planning packages remain off to one side until they become work packages and only then do these work packages show up on my schedule. Even then, they don't show up unless they are meant to be real. In other words, using a checkbook analogy, I want 35 tasking "checks" on my schedule if there are 35 tasking "checks" to process.

I need to mention that both the external (proposal) schedule and the internal (planning) schedule have schedule elements that represent the following:

- Engineering part: Ideally these come from a small set of reusable process elements that have predecessor/successor relationships to other process elements based on engineering principles, designed pieces/parts story, integration planning, and project planning. They do in my approach.
- Contractual part: These are customer-imposed interface meetings, major design review events, deliverable schedules, etc.
- Management part: These are support items, LOE items, internally imposed tasks and events, periodic internal management reviews, etc.

The engineering part is the most uncertain and can't be totally laid out up front. The other two parts can be laid out totally up front with a high degree of certainty that it's correct. Because of this phenomenon, the engineering part can be laid out up to the execution of top-level designs with a high degree of certainty. Top-level design executions gives you the system piece/part story so that you can identify the schedule tasking required. The integration plan can provide you with a tremendous amount of insight into how those pieces/parts get ordered on a schedule along with the integration story.

It must be blatantly obvious to the reader that managing a software project schedule is only as good as the following:

- The workflow represented on that schedule
- The connection of the workers to that workflow

You can manage fiction or you can manage reality. Too many software project managers manage fiction; i.e., what is managed (as per the schedule) has:

■ Little to no relationship to the real end-to-end life-cycle story
■ Little to no relationship to what is really going on in the software engineer's world (i.e., to those actually "working the project").

The first point deals with the key question: "Just how did the software project manager come up with this stuff on the schedule?" I have seen schedule details that look as if they were made up and came from nowhere. I have also seen schedule inputs that came from multiple leads, which had no resemblance to each other in name or level of detail. These inputs just got "plopped" into the schedule. At two separate companies, I actually asked software leads what "Implement Unit" meant on a schedule. The responses I received were scary; for example:

■ "When we get a clean compile, we're done."
■ "After compiling OK we do a quick code walk-through."
■ "After compiling with no errors, we create a little driver and test that code."
■ "We compile and then inspect the code. Then we're done."
■ "After compiling, we integrate our new code with the existing code to see if it hangs together."

My point is that you may have hundreds of "Implement Unit" tasks on your schedule and they may mean different things based on which software lead provided that schedule line item to you! You may be going along believing one thing, whereas other interpretations are also being made. This is just on an implementation kind of task. Can you imagine the possibilities with design-type tasks?

I hope to show you that because this is an important SPM artifact, it needs to be created and managed predicated on an intelligent process basis not by the seat of your pants. I also hope to show you that when you align the schedule with a suitable process model, you align your schedule with both SPM and software development management. You can take advantage of near real-time software project improvements and make life a whole lot simpler for all concerned — including yourself.

For your internal planning schedule, you can only lay out what you know when you do know it! The basic elements of an internal planning schedule are called *tasks* and *events*. Tasks are verb-based, indicating actions to be done. Events are noun-based. These schedule elements have predecessor/successor relationships to other schedule line items. Tasks produce one or more work products to signify "done." Tasks work on objects. Tasks get assigned to real people, along with a responsible task lead, when executed. When completed, a schedule has lots and lots of tasks and events all strung together, representing the end-to-end workflow. Related tasks and events can be rolled up into noun-based summaries. You can even have summaries of summaries to achieve varying levels of detail in a schedule to accommodate different audiences. Practitioners are supposed to work the low-level tasks (I say "supposed to" because in many companies the schedule is looked at by the software project manager and the real work is done by some other mechanism!). Project management likes higher-level summaries because it provides a macro view to upper management and to external customers. It is that workflow detail that you are managing, however. I cannot overemphasize enough that it is the internal plan or schedule that is used for planning and tracking. This has the real-world tasking shown along with rolled-up summaries and provides a low-level roadmap of things that need to be done.

Think about it: the schedule is the real work driver for schedulable things. Later in this book, I will address all the nonschedulable things via the process model. The schedule indicates, what you need to do — not how you are to do it. I intend to show you that once you directly connect schedule tasking "whats" to process "whats," there are many marvelous benefits.

Unfortunately, I have seen my share of internal planning schedules that have a mix of verb-based and noun-based tasks along with variable task semantics (mentioned earlier), depending on who submitted them to the software project manager. I have also seen that most companies have no such schedule–process connection at all! I will show you that with my described method, you totally eliminate this ambiguity and significantly improve task repeatability. Figure 2.2 shows this internal planning type of schedule.

You will notice that for purposes of illustration I have shown completed tasks differently from noncompleted tasks. I have also shown only a fragment, using design tasks as an example. In reality, I suggest you use the checkbook method to indicate task completion.

Merely add a column in your schedule to check off tasks that are done — as you would do for check reconciliation. One place I worked had huge schedule charts plastered on the walls throughout the company with an elaborate color-coding system for completed tasks versus noncompleted tasks. The concept of "now" was a pen on a dangling string moved across the schedule. If a task was completed on or before the designated time, it was colored green. If a task was not completed, it was colored red. The software project manager would be verbally beaten up, depending on how much red showed up! Schedule updates were a group-grope session on a weekly basis. It was no wonder that people were not lining up to be software project managers at this place.

As you read further, you will see that I make the case that life-cycle phases, as described by each PAD from the process repository, are possible summaries for scheduling. I will also show you why they don't make sense for progress reporting. Later on, I will introduce you to process activities that become schedule task instances and activity groups that are used for progress reporting. At this stage, you might be shaking your head about PADs, activities, and activity groups. I'll explain all that later and clear it up for you.

The Project Management Plan (PMP) Document

For many years, the government forced contractors to provide an actual document called the PMP. This document even required a complete format outline of what had to be included, as described in a data item description (DID). Many project managers had to "cut and paste" a schedule into this document to satisfy the government. This violated basic database rules because we now had two copies of the schedule — one real and one inside the PMP. Over time, which one do you believe? The government put two buckets of information into a single document container — stuff from a schedule and stuff beyond a schedule.

There are some things that need to be part of a PMP document that are not available via a project schedule. These are, for example:

- Risks
- Process basis for this project
- Test environment
- Software and environment descriptions

If you use a process-based approach to SPM, much of that information is already documented in the process repository and does not need to be documented again. It is a big mistake to cut and paste schedule stuff into this document. Resist the urge to do this. Make reference to your schedule as your plan. I can't tell you how many times I have observed that the PMP is considered as "something to be done" and then shelved rather than be used as a real plan. It was always unbelievable to me that some people have this attitude. Here's a novel approach — use a plan as a plan! In my approach, the combination of schedule (the major plan) and the associated topics in the PMP become the basis for the software project managers to do their job as well as serve as the basis for quality audits and compliance. I will show you later that plans are an incredible multipurpose work product that you really will want to use — especially with the described layered process framework architecture. I will show you that plans are truly the drivers of work rather than something to be done and ignored. I will also show you the benefits of a "virtual document" so that you don't violate database concepts and don't waste time in the actual document preparation business. You have enough to do without being an English major and a document specialist.

Planning the Software Project

At the beginning of the execution segment of your project, you have the proposal-time schedule, which should include the following:

- All the contract requirements embedded in the schedule
- All the deliverables identified in the schedule
- All the support level of effort (LOE) stuff identified in the schedule

What you don't have primarily involves the following engineering part of the schedule:

- The development life cycle representation in the schedule. This may have been alluded to at the proposal time.
- The system piece/part tasking story — because we're not there yet.
- The schedule task ordering — because there is no integration plan yet.
- Probably also all the internal management stuff (e.g., internal reviews).

Plans are not static. Plans need revisions and updating for things such as the following:

- Better visibility
- Customer requirements changes
- Changes in subcontractor work assignments
- Process rework

In this described approach, plans are naturally extended (or changed) as we get better visibility on the system pieces/parts and tasking ordering. Customer requirement changes, if significant, almost always require pruning of entire schedule branches of tasks for the future revisit of those tasks. In my approach, we can actually tag these pruned and relocated task branches (via the charge number) as rework. The most cosmetic change to a plan involves changes in assignments within your organization. Changes in subcontractor work assignments can also be cosmetic if your subcontractor is aligned with your charge numbering system — otherwise, it may take some time to reassign tasks across separate companies. Process-based rework is the worst of all. This means you are forced into rework because your process basis has failed you. This rework reason hits at the heart of your SEPG (software engineering process group) efforts and could affect your whole institution.

Traditional Conversion of Planning Packages to Work Packages

This SPM concept can be the biggest mistake anyone can do when practicing software project management. The idea is that at estimation planning time, we know we want to do certain things, but, because no real designing has been done, we can only identify big chunks of future work (called *planning packages*) and break them up later (into *work packages*) as we get a better idea of what really needs to be done. This assumes that what you estimated earlier equals what you are really doing later! How stupid that is! At execution time, you usually have no idea how these planning package chunks were derived:

- Was it from something real?
- Was it an educated guess?
- Was it off the wall?

Then to add insult to injury, we now try to fit what we're really doing to this fantasy!

My advice to any software project manager is, "don't do that."

Unfortunately, there are software project managers out there who think that a schedule can represent what you think it will be (planning) and "mark off" work as it's done (tracking). The traditional planning schedule and tracking schedule tend to be two separate threads because traditional thinking tries to compare how we're doing in relation to some base position. The thinking prevails that because we don't know all things up front, we can be very general in our planning and create planning-type summaries called planning packages to represent work to be done. As we get better visibility of what really needs to be done, we can subdivide these planning packages to create a set of work packages (also known as tasks). This is where, hopefully, real work is done.

What I have just said is the traditional way of doing SPM. The problem with this traditional approach is that earlier estimates are almost never equal to the real work unfolding during execution! I worked at one place where the project manager had a fit because the design type of planning package identified three subsystems — yet the actual design came up with four subsystems. His tantrums were so bad that the designers forced the number of subsystems to be three — even though it resulted in a bad design. Software project managers need to really understand that an estimate is an estimate — period. Allow the actual design to be what it should be. Take lessons learned and fold them into your next project's estimate — don't force them into this one. Estimations primarily drive estimated costs, which, in turn, drive contract bid pricing. Both are past history. You have a built-in motivation for getting better estimates. You won't stay in business long without doing this!

This is one area in which I will show the reader what some may consider an unconventional approach to SPM. I make no effort to mark off fictional planning packages representing earlier estimations that include all the time, effort, and aggravation of variance reporting. In an ideal software development world, your estimates are so "on" that they match the later reality of execution. Dream on! By not doing this, I eliminate all the aggravation of trying to make sense of two (possibly dissimilar) metrics. I never want to superimpose any piece/part story at estimation time when executing a project. I will also show you that execution tasks are never to be placed on a project schedule unless they are real. Traditional software project managers may have a lot of trouble with this thinking, but most people will agree that it makes sense. I do advocate using the process itself as the implied set of planning packages. Stay tuned to see how all this works effortlessly, given the described process underpinning.

Tracking the Software Project

You can't track what you didn't plan correctly! That would be akin to having 26 entries in your checkbook, with 35 checks to be accounted for (or tracked)! Unfortunately, many of the software project managers I've worked with didn't really understand this fundamental concept. The plan part is built on sand for many project managers. You can never track a project when your plan basis is a pile of best guesses of what you think might happen versus what really is going to happen. With this process-based SPM approach, I hope to convince the readers that my method does not allow figments of anyone's imagination to show up on any plan. Also, I will show that the planning basis is rooted in process and endorsed by engineering. Remember, engineering are the folks who are doing the real work. That powerful partnership provides a plan that does reflect reality for actual work and for project tracking. If you have 35 checks to be accounted for, you'll have 35 entries in your checkbook.

Traditionally, to track any software project assumed that you had something to track against! That something was, for the most part, the time-based project plan expressed by your planning schedule. The thought was that if you have a garbage plan, you have garbage tracking. There was no point in even discussing software project tracking if your plan was bogus. If the project plan was incomplete by missing some work elements, you could not successfully track that project.

Historically, many software project managers took the planning schedule, made up of lots of planning packages, and decomposed these planning packages into work packages or schedule tasking as visibility dictated. Once this was done, they could assign work packages (tasks) to be done and check them off as work is done. The problem with this is that the planning packages seldom, if at all, matched reality once execution started.

Tracking involves initiating work elements or tasks in a structured way to create work products that signify "done" for any task. Once done, you can mark these off the list of things to be done and get on with the next task at hand. As each task is marked off, you can update any of your earned value calculations to show progress and revise things such as budgeted work performed, performance indicators, and estimated time to complete (ETC) calculations.

All this works great if your original schedule is great. It is horrible if your schedule does not reflect the reality of the work tasks. Ideal tracking has a 1:1 relationship to designated tasks on a software project schedule. Unfortunately, I have seen more examples than I care to admit of plan schedules not aligning with real-world tasks. If that happens, it is extremely difficult (if not impossible) to provide effective progress indicators against a fictional plan.

I will probably shock my readers at this point and suggest a totally different way of doing this that is simpler, process based, and makes sense. I advocate a planning/tracking approach that uses the process execution itself to drive the planning schedule for effective tracking. My approach actually uses design results for all of the following:

- Be an input to further target designs/implementations (norm).
- Drive the project schedule so that tasks reflect reality.
- Drive the software configuration management project repository structures.
- Drive charge number expansion.

In addition, my approach places a heavy dependence on the integration plan to:

- Identify pieces/parts for integration planning.
- Dictate task ordering on your schedule.

I hope to show you that once you have a process-based SPM approach, you will get that alignment automatically for real progress indicators.

The traditional way to report progress is time based. This method does not consider all tasks the same but looks at completed tasks based on a calendar. Each task is taken on its own merit for the duration. Traditional SPM tends to favor this method. I hope to convert you from doing business this way. It is certainly one method of progress reporting but is complicated and quite often meaningless. It does have a lower granularity than what I'm going to propose. As a software development manager, asking people where they were and getting a response that 80 percent of the work has been done is a useless piece of information. It's possible that the first 80 percent was really easy and the last 20 percent is going to take 5 times longer. Many software project managers use the unit-of-time based way of reporting progress.

Let's look at the scenario from Figure 2.2 as an example. We have a set of design tasks on a schedule as follows:

- "Design Down (system)" is done and took 2 time units (e.g., weeks).
- "Design Down (subsystem A)" is done and took 1.5 time units.
- "Design Unit (AA)" is not done and will take 1 time unit.
- "Design Unit (AB)" is not done and will take 1.5 time units.
- "Design Down (subsystem B)" is done and took 2 time units.
- "Design Unit (BA)" has not started and is a 1-time-unit item
- "Design Unit (BB)" has not started and is a 2-time-unit item.
- "Design Unit (BC)" has not started and is a 2-time-unit item.

The reporting information is as follows:

- Total tasks = 8
- Completed tasks = 3
- Total time units = 13
- Completed time units = 5.5

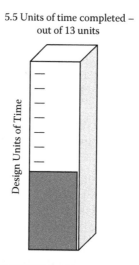

Figure 2.3   **Progress by time-unit completion method.**

The time-unit method of reporting progress is shown in Figure 2.3.

There is no question that time-based reporting is, on one hand, of a finer granularity than activity-based reporting. On the other hand, each unit of time may not reflect the real progress. As an example, I had a new fence put in. I knew how many fence posts had to go in. I also knew from the first post that each post took a certain amount of time to install. Unexpectedly, we ran across a huge rock seam where one posthole was to go. The amount of time for that post was several orders of magnitude greater than all the others. If we had counted progress for 10 posts at 90 percent for the easy posts, we would have no clue as to real progress because the last 10 percent took as much as all the other 9 combined. I quote this method as a widely used method of reporting progress. I am advocating a different method, as described in the text that follows.

3 tasks completed –
out of 8 tasks

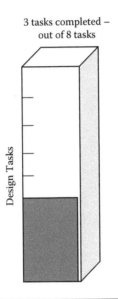

Figure 2.4   Progress by task completion method.

A really simple way (but not as exact) is to consider each task as a reportable unit, being the same as any other task. We know that this is not exactly true, because a top-level design might be considerably shorter than a lower-level detail design. Statistically, however, over the life of a project, it doesn't matter. To show this comparison, let's view each task as weighted the same as any other task. This provides a really easy way to communicate progress: merely count the "done" tasks as compared to the overall number of tasks contained in that summary. This is the task (activity) method of reporting progress; Figure 2.4 depicts this simpler method.

You will notice that these progress management indicators are not that different; however, with this latter method, it is absolutely simple to derive these metrics. Simply add up the tasks belonging to the metric topic (in our case, "design"), and every time you complete a task you count "1" as a "done" count. What could be simpler! I will show you that the simpler method is far superior and yet easier once we head toward an activity or task-based scheduling method. Don't complicate SPM unnecessarily.

PROCESS FRAMEWORK ARCHITECTURE

Chapter 3

Process Overview

Introduction

At this point, the reader is probably asking what a process architectural foundation has to do with software project management (SPM). After all, you map out tasks on a project schedule, based on past experience and software engineering practices. Your organization has piles of procedural "how-to" processes along with document templates, forms, and various checklists in their process repository. Engineers check the work, and the organization produces all the necessary documents for any project. What's the problem?

I do realize that for many people the word "process" is a four-letter word. Unfortunately some of my process colleagues have lost sight of the fact that process is there to support the organization — not the other way around. Many companies have piles and piles of processes that are not connected to anything but are there because of the possibility that there may be some tidbits of value to someone — if they could find it.

Here's an action item if you feel you have that situation:

- Take a functional area of your company.
- Identify all the process elements that relate to that functional area.
- Draw a box for each process element and name it — all on a single page.
- Draw a line from each reference to its referenced box.

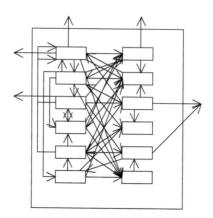

Figure 3.1   Process "spaghetti chart" for process failures.

Is it clean or is it a "spaghetti chart?" If it's similar to Figure 3.1, you need major surgery on your process basis. This chart actually represents "subcontract management" at one company where I worked! I personally took paper copies of all subcontract-management-related process elements home over a weekend and drew this picture. The middle was a blob of black. I presented this to company executives on Monday morning and told them that this was why they're having subcontractor management problems! No one in his right mind could possibly follow this — even if they wanted to!

If you are experiencing the following problems, they are also strong indicators that you need underlying process architecture:

- Schedules being missed by a large margin
- Rework being a large percentage of the developmental life cycle
- Product quality and reliability being low or questionable
- Defects being primarily found at test time
- People working excessive hours — tired, creating defects
- No consistency for tasks and work products
- Lack of configuration management control on developmental work products
- Quality emphasis being focused on testing
- Chaotic, firefighting mode of operation generally
- Excessive thrashing on internal releases between test and engineering

Having raised all these factors, it is now important to note the standards that any process solution has to meet; these are:

- An end-to-end repeatable solution for any development life cycle
- A methodology that supports both schedule estimation and execution
- Flexibility and extensibility at the how-to level for inter- or intraproject and project-scale variances
- A methodology that supports built-in quality gates throughout the life cycle
- A methodology that supports metrics collection
- A methodology that supports process audits
- A methodology that supports process improvements
- A methodology that is role based to show process involvement
- A methodology that produces standard work products
- A methodology that is easy to use

For a software project manager, in particular, there are many reasons why a process-based approach to SPM is important:

- Short process basis determination for a project.
- Better and better planning estimations of work.
- Accurate internal planning schedule for effective tracking.
- Shortened time to market (TTM).
- Easier earned value calculations.
- Direct partnership with accounting, software configuration management (SCM), and software quality assurance (SQA).
- Deterministic metric data collection.
- Total alignment with process improvements for your project.
- Seamless engineering staffing from one project to another.
- It's just easier!

Let's take a look at some of these benefits for a software project manager now. I will deal with these topics in much more detail in this section of the book.

A big killer of any project is the cost of errors. We all understand the value of compounding when it relates to interest received on a savings account. That's a good thing. Compounding also happens with defects — except it's negative compounding for any software project manager. Defects introduced early in the life cycle (and not detected) have a huge compounding effect on defects later in the life cycle. Over time, those compounded defects get more and more expensive to fix. The trick is to catch and fix defects as early as possible, while

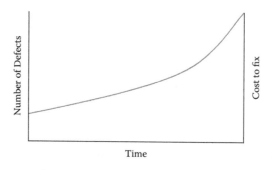

Figure 3.2 Defect-compounding effect.

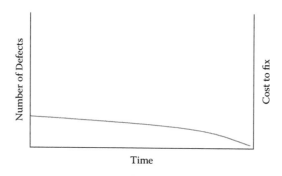

Figure 3.3 Early-defect detection effect.

they are still cheap to fix and have not started compounding the errors. We can see this defect-compounding effect graphically in Figure 3.2.

Unfortunately, many companies experience this phenomenon and address this by having SQA people obtain quality via testing at the end of the life cycle. That quality focus is too little too late. This SQA involvement is the little "q" of quality. From an SPM perspective, massive defects at test time can torpedo the project. You see this manifested in the thrashing and churning between your engineering group and your test group that can reach a point at which the developmental impact on your SPM agenda can be horrendous.

You want to head to a process solution that catches defects early, while they're inexpensive and, ideally, have system test be a nonevent. You need to consciously include quality gates into each and every task for that very reason. This is the big "Q" of quality. The described process model gives huge importance to meeting this quality objective. This effect is shown in Figure 3.3.

This process model emphasizes inspections on work products throughout the life cycle. The process model does recognize that not all work products are created equal. Some need stringent inspections. Some don't. The efficiency of the inspection procedure is the single-most important procedure that any software project manager can have in his or her arsenal. As a "process guy," I have certainly run into horrible review or inspection procedures. I have also experienced situations in which this procedural element is somebody's "baby" and he or she is not about to have it changed or replaced — even though it is totally useless! I know; I've been there. At one large cellular telecommunications company, I had a supportive boss and was able to replace their existing inspection and review procedure with a Web-based solution that was all of the following:

- More efficient for accessibility and usage
- Up to ten times faster
- Provided higher-quality inspections than before
- Provided multisite inspector capability
- Provided both defect detection and defect prevention capability
- Built into the entire life cycle

This new inspection method sold itself. The practitioners loved it. The managers loved it. Other divisions in the company wanted it because word-of-mouth endorsements work wonders in any organization. I cannot overemphasize how much the inspection procedure is fundamental to this described approach, and it needs to be such that your workers use it because it works for them. If you have an inspection procedure that has all the bells and whistles but is not used, get rid of it.

You may not have given much thought to the impact a layered process architecture has on SPM. As a software project manager, you want people assigned to your project who can go in running. You simply can't afford a workforce that is wasting (your) project time. If you're a ship's captain, you want your sailors to be able-bodied seamen — not landlubbers! My point is that a layered process architecture that is tightly coupled to your schedules and institutionalized in your organization provides trained people for you. You end up with a seamless engineering, SCM, SQA, and accounting support for your project, which can readily move from project to project with little to no special training. That also applies to any software project manager moving from one project to another. How's that for cost savings? You want your training to look similar to Figure 3.4.

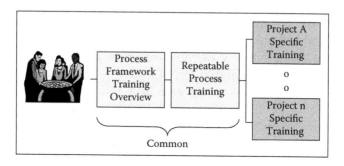

Figure 3.4 Desired process training flow.

With this process architecture institutionalized, you provide all employees with overview training on the process framework architectural model itself, followed by detailed training on the life-cycle connection to the processes. In this model, I advocate inspection procedure training as part of the common training. These types of training courses are common to all hands. The only project-specific training that might apply is in the use of a particular process element that is to be employed on that project. There may be other project-specific training needs related to tool usage, etc., or specialized training to successfully execute certain activities (e.g., requirements normalization and clarification training). I hope the reader can readily see that moving employees from one project to another becomes really easy because of the process basis.

The problem, in a nutshell, is that the very essence of "what you need to do" tasks are not represented on a 1:1 basis in your process repository. If I have a design-type task versus an integrate task, what are the inputs, steps, outputs, etc., for one task lead versus another task lead? Do I just assume that everyone knows what they're doing and cross my fingers for repeatability and success? Many do just that!

I should be able to close my eyes, point to any task at random on the project schedule, and:

- Relate that task to a process "what we need to do" activity for "what" level information, such as:
  - Task dependencies.
  - Inputs to this task.
  - High-level "what you have to do" steps to complete this task. This provides the linkage to the "how-to" world.
  - Outputs from this task.

- Roles involved in getting this task done.
- Training involved to do this task.
- Metrics involved in this task.
- Task estimates.
▪ Relate that task to predecessor or successor tasks based on a process life cycle.

I should also be able to pull out any one of the "how-to" procedures and get a satisfactory answer to the "where does this fit in the life cycle?" question. If you can't answer this, you are an organization with piles of process stuff out there, and that's all. "How-to" elements should be tied to one (or more) of these "what" anchors, i.e.:

▪ High-level "what" steps inside any activity as an elaboration of that "what"
▪ High-level "what" requirements in any international standard that you're following (e.g., ISO9001)
▪ High-level "what" requirements in any government regulation that you're following (e.g., FAA, FDA, etc.)
▪ High-level "what" pseudo requirements in any maturity model that you're following (e.g., CMMI)
▪ High-level "what" requirements from the company policies that you're following

Elaborated "how-to" procedures tied to activities are directly tied to places in the life cycle via the process activity diagrams (PADs). The others are event-driven procedures that are also tied to the life cycle by virtue of being global (e.g., corrective action) or by being segment or phase dependent (e.g., requirements changes and internal builds). This book will focus on the elaborated ones tied to activities and touch on all the others because of the book's perspective on SPM. I will discuss these topics in more detail later.

If you had a process architecture that provided all of these:

▪ "What you had to do" process elements separated from "how you need to do it" process elements.
▪ These "what" process elements were self-contained and provided everything you needed to know about doing that "what-level" process element.
▪ These same "what" process elements showed you all the valid predecessor and successor "what" elements for the end-to-end story.

- These same "what" process elements could be identified within life-cycle phases.
- These same "what" process elements were grouped under umbrella terms.

Then, you would end up with SPM schedules made up of:

- Consistent "what-level" descriptions directly tied to your process world for high-process repeatability; i.e., a drag-and-drop approach to schedule tasks from a process-based "pick list" of "what you have to do" activities.
- Consistent predecessor and successor relationships based on your process life-cycle roadmap of "what-level" tasks — not based on individual leads.
- Consistent task umbrella terms for SPM metrics.
- Built-in SCM controls for each "what-level" task appropriate to that task's outputs; i.e., you eliminate the problem of the "what level of CM control is needed?" question. It's built-in.
- Built-in quality gates for each "what-level" task that places quality responsibility on the producer — not the consumer. The questions of "what templates do I use?" and "where are the inspection checklists or examples?" are eliminated. It's built-in. This reduces later (and expensive) defects.
- Consistent inputs by "what-level" task. The questions of "what do I need to do this task?" along with "where do I get it?" are eliminated. It's built-in.
- Consistent outputs by "what-level" task. The questions of "what gets produced?" and "where do they go?" are eliminated. It's built-in.
- Consistent role assignments per "what-level" task. This is a definite aid to SPM and development management for task assignments to get the right mix of people performing the job for success.
- Consistent metrics data collection per "what-level" task. Metrics data collection is built into the process activity and, thus, to the schedule task. It virtually eliminates pushback for metrics data collection because it's an integral part of "doneness" for the task.
- Consistent special training requirements per "what-level" task. This is also a definite aid to SPM and development management to make sure that special training needs have been handled for task success.

■ Consistent dependencies per "what-level" task. These address things such as "is the test lab in place and set up?" kinds of dependencies. Again, tying this to process activities (and thus tasks) makes sure that all things are in place for success.

■ Schedule tasks that developers, SCM, quality, accounting, and SPM work and manage. There is absolutely no reason for multiple schedules. Developers are connected to tasks (and, thus, process activities) for "what you need to do" instructions along with "how-to" hooks to get the job done. Accounting manages the enfolding charge numbers assigned to tasks. You achieve total repeatability for development efforts. SCM hooks are present to make sure the correct level of configuration control is being used. Quality is built-in by quality gate inspections along with total auditability of task completion built into this model. SPM manages task completions for earned value calculations.

What this means is that the SPM world is directly connected to the software development world, the software quality world, the SCM world, and the accounting world. All are connected to the process world with these awesome benefits:

■ Software process improvements can be included in your projects close to real-time if you so choose.

■ Software process improvements drive all SPM schedules for total consistency across the enterprise.

■ Time charges can be directly tied to process "what-level" activities for better project estimations based on prior actual data.

■ Earned value calculations can be based on activity or task granularity for simplicity.

■ Software developer work elements are identical to SPM work elements, period!

■ All process elements are auditable for quality checking. Audits can be done by anyone in the spirit of the ISO 9001 definition of "quality."

■ SCM is built into the process "what you need to do" world that shows up as schedule tasks.

■ Very high level of process repeatability because tasks and process activities are the same.

■ Software subcontractor management can be much cleaner because all the "whats" need doing, regardless of what badge is being worn. Only the "how-tos" are different (along with tool variations).

- Project-specific "how-to" processes can be incorporated into the process "how-to" pool of selectable procedures. This encourages better mousetraps.
- The process basis for any project is the set of process "what-level" activities along with "how-to" selections. This can be accomplished in minutes for quality auditing and project execution.

I will now describe a process framework model architecture that makes SPM so much better. I will concentrate on those aspects of the process architecture pertinent to SPM. For a full description of this architecture, see Reference 1. I have written this book such that you will not need any reference to understand what I'm getting at to perform SPM successfully using a process-based model. This book is intended to be self-contained.

The Software Process Framework Model Overview

Let me introduce the reader to the overall process architecture "pyramid." See Figure 3.5, which shows the user view of the major layers of process elements in this process framework architectural model.

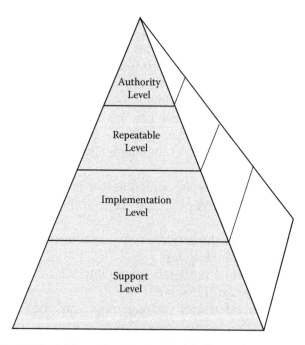

Figure 3.5 Process architecture "pyramid."

The model layers are broken down into four major levels of process elements as follows:

- Authority level: This level contains all the reasons why we're doing this in the first place. The following types of things go in here:
  - International standards (e.g., ISO 9001) requirements. These are the top-level "shall" statements that you must follow if you are ISO certified. For example, ISO 9001 has a standard requirement that states: "The supplier shall have a corrective action system." This top-level "what" requirement can be directly connected with your "corrective action" procedural element as its reason for being.
  - Maturity model (e.g., Capability Maturity Model for Software [SW-CMM], Capability Maturity Model Integration [CMMI]) "requirements." Although the "M" stands for "model," these are, for all intents and purposes, real requirements. Most companies involved with CMMI consider these as pseudo requirements even though it's not a standard but a model.
  - Government regulations to be followed. This is for those regulated industries that are required to follow FDA, FAA, etc., regulations. Similar to ISO 9001, top-level government regulations are "what" requirements that need connectivity to something in your process arsenal.
  - Company policies to be followed. These are company-specific policies to be followed. Usually these are low in number, but they are still requirements that have to be followed. Writing company policies in a vacuum makes no sense unless these get connected to something in the process repository that actually fulfills those policies.
- Repeatable level: This level contains all the "what you have to do" processes. I call these "activities." This level also includes end-to-end life-cycle story representations of those "what" elements. These are a collection of PADs that, when strung together, form a life cycle. This level connects the process world to the project schedule world and is the single-most important level for any software project manager.
- Implementation level: So called because this is where the "rubber meets the road" for all the "how-to" procedures that elaborate on elements in the two layers mentioned earlier. Many say this is where the real work happens. In this model, I

introduce a concept called the "how selector" to provide that flexibility and extensibility for "how-tos." "How-to" procedural selectability address project scalability differences, site differences, and tool set differences that occur in the real world. Almost nothing in life has only one way of doing things. This model accommodates that philosophy.

■ Support level: This level contains all the information about work products and forms, including templates, quality checklists, guidelines, coding standards, and examples. You will understand later why I place a big emphasis on quality checklists for not only detecting defects but also for providing a mechanism for defect prevention. I use these checklists to achieve software process improvements throughout any life cycle.

In this process model, I do not allow process elements to just "be there." All process elements are connected to something above it in the pyramid. If you ever have a process element by itself, get rid of it. I also have stringent rules for that connectivity:

■ "Whats" flow down to "how-to's" and support items.
■ "How-to's" flow down to support items.

This connectivity is shown in Figure 3.6.

The big thing to notice is you can break down the real-world usage of process into two groups:

■ Schedulable things
■ Nonschedulable things

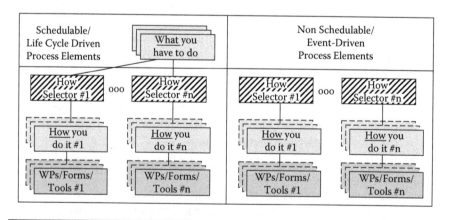

Figure 3.6 The real-world what/how connection.

The schedulable world has a "what you have to do" aspect that becomes that end-to-end life cycle manifested onto a project schedule. The nonschedulable world does not have that layer. No matter what, both have a set of selectable "how-to" procedures that, in turn, are associated with work products, forms, tools, etc. Both schedulable and nonschedulable process elements have a connection to some part of any life cycle. The schedulable activities (or task instances) are explicit members of a designated phase within any given life cycle (e.g., "Design Down" activity is within the "design" phase). The nonschedulable event-driven procedures have a less granular connection with a life cycle. These event-driven procedures can be:

- Global to the entire life cycle (e.g., corrective action, process assessments, etc.)
- Associated with a life-cycle segment (pre-execution versus execution) (e.g., requirements changes)
- Associated with a life-cycle phase (e.g., design phase)

Any reverse connectivity associated with Figure 3.6 (i.e., traceability) is accomplished via compliance matrices. Your assessors, auditors, and SEPG folks mostly use these.

With this process activity–schedule task connection along with event-driven procedure connections to the life cycle, you are completely in the loop for process improvements as close to real-time as you want. This loop is shown in Figure 3.7.

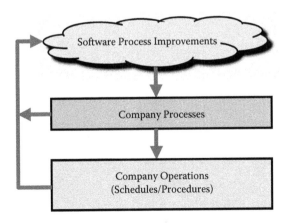

Figure 3.7   The software process improvement loop.

For this book, I will concentrate mainly on the repeatable level and, thus, the schedulable part. This is the portion of the process repository that directly connects the process world to the wonderful world of SPM project schedules. If the reader wants a full understanding of the whole architectural model, I recommend my earlier book [1], in which I not only address this view but also the other sides of the pyramid model (e.g., where training packages fit).

Chapter 4

Life-Cycle Mapping

Introduction

It is extremely important that you map your process activities into phases of a life cycle. As a reminder, process activities become task instances on a project schedule and represent the "what you need to do" process elements. As a "process guy," I have been absolutely amazed at what some companies do with their processes. Some examples are as follows:

- They do nothing. "We just know what we're doing." These are the companies that don't last long. I just love this one.
- They have a sparse set of things that people can use if they want to and if they can find it. This is the "hide-and-seek" approach to process.
- They have a horrendous pile of stuff with overlapping documentation and variations on any given topic. This is the "good luck to you" approach in getting anything done.
- They have a pile of process elements with no consistency and no architecture. Pick out whatever you think applies. The "whats," "hows," and "policies" are all mixed in with each other. This is the "Yeah, we have processes" approach, but no one is using it much.
- Major functional areas of the company organize processes. This is the guaranteed "stovepipe" approach to processes and is far

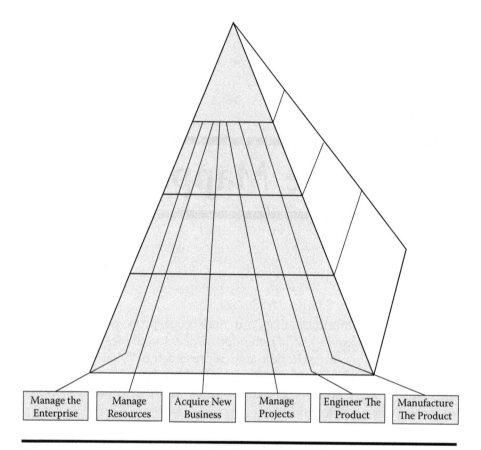

Manage the Enterprise	Manage Resources	Acquire New Business	Manage Projects	Engineer The Product	Manufacture The Product

Figure 4.1   Nonlife-cycle stovepipe approach to process.

from real-world considerations. Possibilities of dangling references (or arrows) are excellent between functional areas. This is the "I know what I do — I don't care what you do" approach to process.

■ My choice — Processes are mapped to life cycles no matter what roles are involved. This is the process-schedule approach to process. This directly supports intergroup coordination.

If you have the stovepipe approach, it would be similar to slicing the process pyramid shown in Figure 3.5 to arrive at Figure 4.1.

The functional areas shown in this figure shows the way that one company actually did this and then wondered why they ended up with stovepipe processes by functional area of the company. The only alignment they achieved was that they had separate vice presidents in charge of each functional area and each could claim a set of processes as his or her own. This particular company selected the following major categories to map processes:

■ Manage the enterprise.
■ Manage resources.
■ Manage projects.
■ Acquire new business.
■ Engineer the product.
■ Manufacture the product.

It turned out that the first three bulleted items were exclusively event-driven "how-to" procedures that really supported the last three items. The last three bulleted items really do have some kind of life-cycle basis. They mixed apples and oranges and ended up with no connectivity to any project schedule. You quite often have a senior manager who has put his or her job on the line behind this approach. If someone such as me steps into this environment and tries to change it to a life-cycle process mapping, the pushback can be enormous. Dealing with abortion, religion, or homosexual rights would be a cakewalk in comparison!

Life-Cycle Web Representation

I do recognize that some companies have more than one life cycle. They might have a development life cycle and a product support life cycle, for example. These enterprises need a super top-level Web site that directs users to the correct life cycle for their project. For software engineering companies that do software development using developmental model variations, you can use the same process life-cycle representation for all of the following:

■ Waterfall software development model
■ Iterative software development model
■ Spiral software development model

The activity selection criterion on a schedule decides the development model for execution purposes. Think of selectable activities as magnets that you can organize on a board. The ways they are laid out make it a spiral model versus an iterative model versus a waterfall model.

You might see something similar to Figure 4.2 if you have this multiple life-cycle situation.

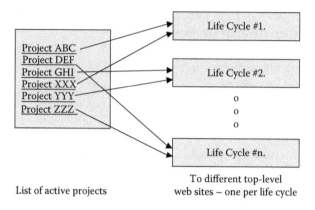

List of active projects

To different top-level
web sites – one per life cycle

Figure 4.2 Multiple-life-cycle Web representation.

With an emphasis on mapping processes to a life cycle, it is important to point out that the real world of process execution can be broken down into two distinct areas of interest as follows:

- Schedulable process elements: These are the ones that show up on your project schedule. These are the ones that you use for both proposal-time planning and execution-time planning and tracking. The schedulable process element is the process activity that resides in one (or more) life-cycle phases.
- Nonschedulable process elements: These are the event-driven asynchronous type of procedures that either just "show up" or are done on a periodic basis. The nonschedulable process element is the how-to procedure whose scope can exist at the phase, segment, or life-cycle level.

Both need to be represented on your Web-based life-cycle mapping representation. Figure 4.3 shows the general method I've used to address both these worlds.

Let's look at this figure and break it down into its component parts. Some readers may disagree with my terms and are free to use their own terminology. It is meant to be a one-stop shopping place for the life-cycle story:

- The top part is merely a two-layer table of hyperlinks into various parts of the process repository. People get really upset if they are somewhere in the Web hierarchy after drill downs and have to do back–back–back and link–link–link to get somewhere else. Make this a common table for all your Web pages.

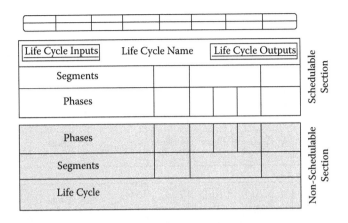

Figure 4.3   General Web layout for any life cycle.

- The big box that follows this table is labeled "Schedulable Section." This is further broken down into three rows:
  - The life-cycle row: This contains the life cycle's name along with the major inputs and outputs to this life cycle.
  - The segment row: This contains the named segments within that life cycle. Examples might be "Pre-execution" and "Execution."
  - The phase row: This contains all the phases within each segment within that life cycle. Examples might be "Requirements," "Design," and "Product Build," etc.
- The bottom box is labeled "Nonschedulable Section." This is also broken down into three rows (except that it is a mirror image of the "Schedulable Section"):
  - The phase row: This contains all the phases within each segment within that life cycle. Within each phase are zero or more links to the event-driven procedures whose scope is at that phase level.
  - The segment row: This contains all the segments within that life cycle. Within each segment are zero or more links to the event-driven procedures whose scope is at that segment level.
  - The life-cycle row: This contains zero or more links to the event-driven procedures whose scope is at that life-cycle level.

I am showing you the format I've used. It is merely one format. You may choose to represent these life-cycle elements in a different

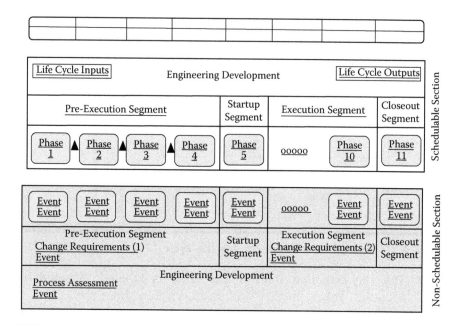

Figure 4.4   Representative life-cycle Web page.

way. Also, this whole format maximizes the use of hyperlinks throughout this life-cycle Web-based representation. The life-cycle process representation of the total end-to-end story is absolutely vital because the project schedule represents the total end-to-end story.

Figure 4.4 shows the same general format but with some more detailed possibilities to help cement in where I'm coming from.

I have no intention of defining a life cycle or its breakdown in this book as a one-size-fits-all kind of solution. What I will do is provide some more examples for you to apply to your own company situation. I have chosen to show only details relevant to software project management (SPM).

There are some points I want to make about this last figure; these are as follows:

■ You will notice that the entire life cycle is identified by the name "Engineering Development." This naming may be a moot point if you have one, and only one, life cycle.
■ You will also notice that I have subdivided this life cycle into these segments:
   – Pre-execution
   – Startup

    – Execution

    – Closeout

You can name your segments similar to this or use different terms.

■ I have also subdivided each segment into one or more named phases. For illustration purposes, the "Pre-execution" segment has been subdivided into four phases:
    – Phase 1
    – Phase 2
    – Phase 3
    – Phase 4

You should be able to recognize that I could have easily substituted other names for these phases such as "Strategic Planning Phase," "Bid Interest Phase," "Bid Pursue Phase," and "Bid Phase," for example.

■ In the "Nonschedulable Section," I have identified the following event-driven procedures:
    – Change requirements: You'll notice I have shown it within the "Pre-execution Segment" as well as the "Execution Segment." If requirements change at proposal time, you need a very different how-to procedure than if requirements change at execution time. That's the reason behind this.
    – Process assessment: You can do this kind of asynchronous event anytime during the entire life cycle. The how-to procedure is the same no matter when this event-driven procedure is executed. That's why it is shown in the life-cycle row.

Clicking on the "Pre-execution Segment" hyperlink would take you to a drill-down Web page representing just that segment. This is shown in Figure 4.5.

This same figure provides that top-level picture of what phases are involved as part of the end-to-end story for pre-execution. You'll notice the inputs and outputs reflect that segment's inputs and outputs — not the entire life cycle.

Clicking on the "Phase 1" hyperlink would take you to a drill-down Web page representing just that phase. This is where you start to see the activity mapping within any given phase. It is this level that shows us the process activities associated with that phase along with all the predecessor/successor relationships either within that phase or with another phase. This is shown in Figure 4.6.

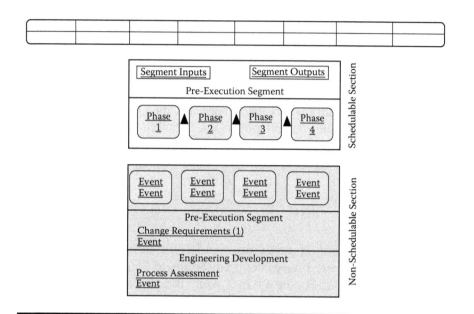

Figure 4.5   Life-cycle segment Web representation.

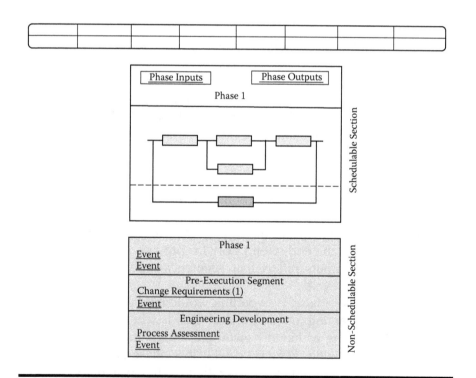

Figure 4.6   Phase Web representation.

You'll notice the inputs and outputs reflect that phase's inputs and outputs. You'll also notice that I've enclosed the activity mappings into an entity that I call the *process activity diagram* or PAD. This is a fairly standard modeling technique used within the software industry (e.g., Unified Modelling Language [UML]). Also notice the dotted line within the PAD. That is what separates "swim lanes." It merely separates main event (or production) activities from support activities. I find that two swim lanes are sufficient for almost all companies. You might find it desirable to color-code support activities differently than production activities. That is also shown in this figure. From this Web page, you can click on any process activity and get all the details about that activity.

Life Cycle/Schedule Connection

In the real world of project schedules, we have tasks that show up in one part of the life cycle whereas others show up at other parts of the life cycle. Design types of tasks do not show up as part of system testing, for example. They show up much earlier in the life cycle — while we're doing design. I hope the reader will agree with me that task placement within a life cycle really does matter. We can really break down any life cycle into chunks (typically called *phases*) and place activities into those life-cycle portions that will become tasks on a schedule. I hope the reader will also recognize that this mapping of activities to a phase is a static thing. We can predetermine what activities go where once, and this can be valid for all usages of those activities.

Engineering practices also give us a really big clue as to what shows up first, second, third, etc. This deals with task connectivity. We do system design before we do subsystem design, before we do unit design, before we do unit coding, etc. A lot of the predecessor/ successor relationships are predetermined as part of normal industry practice. We typically don't code something before we design it (although I worked for one organization that seemed to want to do this a lot to save time — so they said!). I have already established that individual tasks can be contained statically in a life-cycle phase. Now, I'm stating that connections between tasks can also be established statically — both within a phase and between phases. This too can be determined once and be valid for all usages of those tasks.

If we can relate the "what you have to do" schedule tasks to "what you have to do" process activities, we can subdivide any life cycle into phases and map process activities, along with their connections to other activities, in the process world. We can create the entire static end-to-end story across phases for any life cycle. At the high level, we can predetermine:

■ What the set of activities are. These are the schedulable things that can become tasks on a schedule. These are also the selectable "what" elements.
■ What gets "hooked" to what activity, either as a predecessor activity or successor activity.

Consider each schedule task as merely one instance of a process activity. If you had 100 units to code, there would be 100 instances (or tasks) on your schedule of a single process element (or activity) called the "Implement Unit" activity. Similarly, if you had a three-subsystem type of system requiring design at all these levels, you would have four "Design Down" tasks (one for the system level and one for each subsystem) on your schedule but one "Design Down" process activity used for all. For schedule tasks, we add two more pieces of information from the process activity name to make it a task instance; these are as follows:

■ The object being worked (e.g., the system name, the subsystem name, the unit name, etc.)
■ The responsible task lead name

For schedule tasks, the combination of the activity name, object, and responsible person make it an activity instance. I hope the reader will readily see that with this triad it is possible to hyperlink the activity name part directly to your process activity in your intranet process repository! Your schedule tasks are totally connected to your process "what you have to do" activities. There should be no schedule tasks that are "floaters," i.e., not connected to the process world! What a concept! Software process improvements to the process activity can be picked up near real-time on your schedule. This is illustrated in Figure 4.7.

On one implementation, we actually created a schedule template and preloaded all the activity names at the bottom that were already hyperlinked to the respective activity location in the process repository. The software project manager merely selected and dropped each activity into his or her schedule, ending up with all schedule tasks connected to the process description of exactly what needs to be done, etc. This is also shown in the figure.

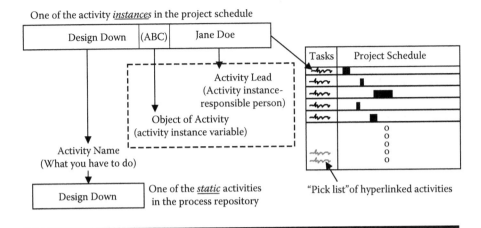

One of the activity _instances_ in the project schedule

Figure 4.7   Schedule/process activity connection.

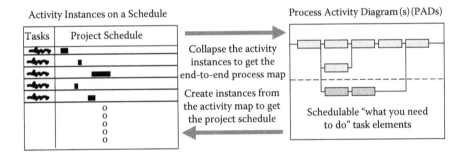

Figure 4.8   Schedule/process activity "morphing."

If we do the activity identification and mapping correctly, we should be able to take all the connected process activities within and across phases depicted in the process world and "morph" them to make any project schedule! Alternatively, we should be able to deduce the process world's representation of activities from any project schedule! When we tie the described process architecture to SPM, we connect software process improvements directly to SPM! To get a firm picture of this morphing phenomenon, see Figure 4.8.

Life-Cycle/Event-Driven Procedure Connection

Although the software project manager's world is primarily focused on scheduled tasks, there are procedural aspects of SPM that he or she will need to know about. We saw these in Figure 4.6. An organization may have how-to procedures related to the following:

- The SPM
- Engineering
- SCM
- SQA
- Data management

These can quite often be as a result of some outside event (e.g., changes in requirements) or may be cyclical by calendar (e.g., every week I am to do ...). It is important that any how-to procedure that needs documenting gets placed in the correct life-cycle scope (phase, segment, or global) and shows up on your life-cycle Web representations.

Although minor in comparison to the scheduled tasks, these event-driven activities can reduce or eliminate defects in the nonscheduled world that you deal with also.

Chapter 5

The Process Activity

Introduction

The process activity is the heart and soul of the real-world connection to software project schedules. The very name of the activity should be verb based because each activity, when executed on a schedule, is itself a high-level "what has to be done" action. The term *action* implies a verb. I cringe when I see schedule tasks shown as nouns or noun-based items. Leave the nouns or noun-based items to the schedule summary description line items or events. For summaries and events, it is appropriate to be a noun or noun-based description.

I hope the reader will agree with me that we can subdivide our entire life cycle into high-level "what has to be done" actions — called *activities*. To proceed, the question now becomes "What constitutes an activity?"

In this process model, I have identified two types of activities:

- The general activity (or just "activity")
- The gate activity

The general activity occurs throughout the entire life cycle and reflects an entity of work to be done. This regular activity has been represented throughout this book as a rectangle within any process activity diagram (PAD). An example of a regular activity is the "Design Unit." The gate activity occurs prior to the execution segment only

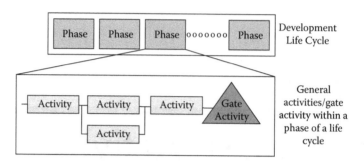

Figure 5.1   Activity connection to a phase.

and reflects a major go/no-go decision point to proceed or not. Some companies use the terms *control gate* or *control point* to reflect these decision points. I like the term *gate* because it really does denote an open–close meaning. You just need to realize that after executing a gate activity, you may stop and not go on at all. This gate activity has been represented throughout this book as a triangle within any PAD prior to the execution segment. An example of a gate activity is "Bid?" When mentioning the word "activity" throughout this book, I am mostly referring to the general form of activity.

Both these types of activities show up inside a PAD. As a reminder, the entire life cycle is subdivided into phases, and each phase contains a PAD of all the activities involved in that phase. This relationship is graphically shown in Figure 5.1.

I will now show you what you need to consider for any action to be an activity (and thus a schedule task instance) as follows:

- It needs to be a logical unit of thought.
- It needs to be a schedulable task, i.e., something that could show up on a project schedule. I purposely used "schedulable" versus "scheduled" because early life-cycle activities (pre-execution time) may or may not be on an actual schedule as the project hasn't started yet.
- It has a defined object when executed; e.g., a "Design Down" activity has a generic object of the system/subsystem piece/part on which you're doing a flow-down design. At execution time, the generic object would be replaced by the real name, e.g., if you were doing a system to subsystem design for system "A," the task description would show "Design Down (A)." A subsystem ABC flow-down design to units would show "Design

Down (ABC)." The activity name is the same; the object at execution time is different.

■ It needs to perform one high-level function, not more; e.g., "Design and Test" are two dissimilar functions that should not be combined into a single activity. The reason here is selectability. See the following item.

■ It needs to be selectable. Activities are atomic elements that you should be able to mix and match in an intelligent fashion on a schedule. "Test Unit" activity, for example, could show up on a schedule for any unit requiring a unit test, but it may be omitted for those units not requiring a unit test.

■ As an atomic element, once placed on a schedule, you should never be allowed to break off in the middle of an activity. You do all steps, not some steps. For a software project manager, that translates to "once assignments are made to an activity instance (or task) and started, you complete that activity instance (or task) totally — no matter what." You never cut it off in the middle. This is a data integrity issue by leaving the activity in a deterministic state.

■ It needs to convey some "value added" function. An activity cannot be something that reads something, and that's all. You need to add something, convert something, etc., to an input to be an activity.

■ It needs to produce one or more work products to signify "done." How can you possibly take earned value on any task if it's unclear what "done" means?

In case there's any "if-then-else" connotation of steps to be done within an activity, you're too low. Also, adjoining activities that always go together should be candidates for combining. Conversely, single activities that take too long could become candidates to become adjoining activities. This last point reflects a reality that may have to exist but has a downside of possibly creating a process defect when implementing as schedule tasks; i.e., you may forget to place the second activity after the first one!

To try to prevent that possible process defect, I suggest you graphically show this situation as per Figure 5.2 to make it abundantly clear that these two activities are tightly connected.

I now hope you recognize that a single activity can provide a wealth of information that can be created by your software engineering process group (SEPG) for an incredibly high level of repeatability when executing projects. You absolutely eliminate project execution problems such as:

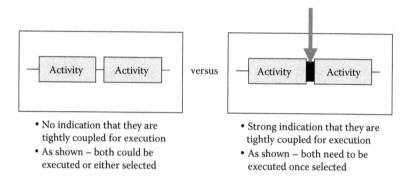

Figure 5.2 Adjoining activities executed together.

- What do I actually do when executing this task?
- What are my inputs? Where are they? What SCM procedure is involved?
- What are my outputs? Where do I place them? What SCM procedure is involved?
- What templates do I use? Where are they?
- What guidelines exist for the work product outputs? Where are they?
- What examples are out there? Where are they?
- What inspection checklists do I need to see to create quality outputs? Where are they?
- What metrics do I need to gather, if any? Who gets these metrics?
- Who do I notify when finished?

These are built-in to the process activity. Because the schedule task is an instance of an activity, all these directives and guidelines are readily available to anyone working that task on a schedule. The power of this is enormous.

There is one more major consideration for activity naming. I have established that activities represent actions and, thus, must be in a "<verb><object>" form. It is highly desirable that all the pre-execution activity names are different from execution activity names. The reason for this is quite simple: pre-execution work is nonpaid overhead work, whereas execution work is paid work. If you really want to get a handle on this nonpaid work to factor into your overhead rates, you'll need to do this. Also, pre-execution activity estimations are based on prior actuals averages, whereas execution-time activities are estimated with that same average but with a loading factor added to account for overhead costs. These estimation factors will be discussed later. A slight variation to the activity name form is to place a "P-" prefix ("P" for Pre-execution) in front of the activity name. You can choose your own method, of course. This comes up mostly in the top-level-design type of activity and requirements types of activities. You do a gross top-level system design at proposal time, and you do a more refined top-level design at execution time. You might want to place the "Design Down" activity in both places, but I can assure you that it complicates activity estimations technique! I recommend you have a "P-Design Down" in the proposal phase (pre-execution segment) and a "Design Down" activity in the design phase (execution segment). Similarly, if you are doing partial requirements clarification at proposal time and more requirements clarifications at execution time, use "P-Clarify Requirements" and "Clarify Requirements," respectively. I will show you why this name separation is important both to this process model and for real-world considerations.

It is worth mentioning again that the ultimate goal is to have all schedule tasks created from a pick-list of process activities. How powerful is that for repeatability! Developers, software leads, quality engineers, SCM, and the software project manager are all reading from the same "sheet of music."

Activity Implementation

From an implementation perspective, you can certainly make an activity as fancy as you want, graphically. However, I found the simplest representation was the best. Figure 5.3 shows a tabular form of a general process activity.

You'll notice that there are two boxes at the top. I found it useful to place hyperlinks there to point to the predecessor activities (left box) and to the successor activities (right box). This allows horizontal traversal through the end-to-end activities in your life cycle. The hyperlinks match the graphical representation in each phase's PAD.

The main box is essentially a two-column table with a header. The header contains the activity name and its generic object names. The left column contains a set of attributes that you'll need when executing this activity on a project schedule. The attributes I've used are given in Table 5.1.

Gate activities have a very identical format as shown in Figure 5.4. The big differences between a gate activity and regular activity are:

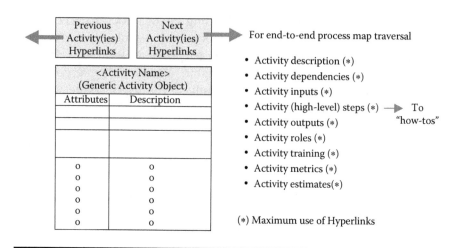

Figure 5.3   Regular activity format.

- A different color (I used red) to clearly distinguish a gate activity from a regular activity.
- Presence of a special high-level step (CONDUCT) that does not show up in regular activities. I will cover these high-level steps later in this chapter.

As this is a Web page, I am a big advocate of keeping verbiage as short as possible. This is not the place to write a treatise on anything. One-liners are better than two. If you really feel the urge to write more, place a "More" hyperlinked tag at the end and take your practitioner to that extra verbiage. People get really upset if you have a scroll bar down the side, and they have to play with it to get to what they want.

The reader will notice that the high-level steps inside an activity provide potential "hooks" to the how-to world. In this model, not all high-level "what" steps require a "how," but every "how" requires a "what." Sometimes the best how-to of all doesn't exist or is a simple mind-jogger checklist kind of thing. I am purposely not getting into the "how-to" model aspects because our focus is on SPM connection to activities. I refer the reader to my earlier book [1] for more details on this subject. Verb-based steps exist inside an activity to fulfill two requirements:

- They are steps that you absolutely and positively want people to do.
- They are important how-to hooks.

Table 5.1 Activity Attributes

Description	This has a one-liner summary description.
Dependencies	This is meant to describe external dependencies such as the presence of a test lab if this was a system-test-type-activity.
Inputs	List of all the generic inputs needed for this activity.
Steps	A list of high-level "what you need to do" steps. Those steps that have a how-to elaboration are hyperlinked to the how-to world. This is the main part of an activity that connects the "whats" to the "hows."
Outputs	List of all the generic outputs created or updated by this activity.
Roles	All the roles involved in the execution of this activity. Suggest hyperlinking each role to a more descriptive role-based list.
Training	Identifies any special training needs to successfully execute this activity. Suggest hyperlinking each training reference to the actual training package.
Metrics	Identifies any metrics to be collected when executing this activity.
Estimates	Reference to prior estimates to execute this activity. Suggest MIN (minimum), AVG (average), L-AVG (loaded average), and MAX (maximum). These will be used by the software project manager for planning and tracking.

It is important to stress again that once an activity is selected and placed on a schedule, all steps are to be executed — not the first four, last three, etc. Although not intuitively obvious, any high-level step can be done when its inputs are there. That might not be obvious because the high-level steps are shown sequentially in any activity. In addition, these high-level steps can all be audited by anyone for quality. See Figure 5.5. This is in keeping with the ISO 9001 concept of quality, which is everybody's responsibility.

I hope the reader will now grasp another incredible benefit with this process connection to SPM: namely, you can embed important "hook" steps to important things. We can now place common steps in each and every activity to address common things such as:

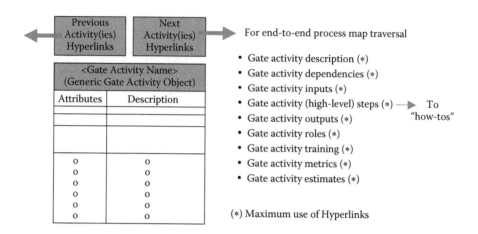

Figure 5.4 Gate activity format.

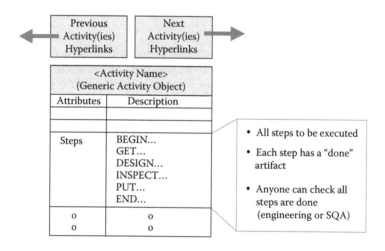

Figure 5.5 Quality perspective for high-level steps.

- Assigning a charge number to this task
- Notifying key players that a task is starting
- Providing a SCM hook in getting input work products out of the project's developmental library
- Giving a quality hook to the inspection procedure as a quality gate
- Providing a SCM hook in getting output work products into the project's developmental library

- Passing off metrics data to whoever gets metrics in your organization
- Notifying key players that a task has finished — for schedule continuity and management plus earned value purposes

I found that these capabilities can be accomplished with these common-to-all-activity high-level steps:

- BEGIN <charge number>
- GET <charge number, filename>
- PUT <charge number, filename>
- CONDUCT <charge number> ** Only used inside gate activities **
- INSPECT <charge number, filename>
- END <charge number>

You may of course choose other verbs. I think these are really simple to grasp as to intent. Most software engineers understand the BEGIN ... END concept. I have applied that same structure to a process activity. Let's look at the SPM value of these steps that are common to all activities (and thus all schedule tasks):

BEGIN: This is a great SPM hook to possibly:
- Let key players know that something is starting. I believe the software project manager is a definite key player, don't you think?
- Assign the charge number to people working this schedule task. Remember, SPM-presented metrics are only as good as work metrics gathered. In Chapter 8, I will show you the power of charge number alignments to process activities.
GET: This too is a great SCM hook to make sure you get the inputs from the right place in the development SCM repository and placed in your activity's "sandbox." Again, if this is not done properly, you suffer from the "garbage-in-garbage-out" syndrome. This is also a great SCM how-to hook for the correct procedural element for this part of the life cycle. You eliminate the SCM level of control question totally at execution time. That's powerful.
PUT: This is another great SCM hook to make sure you place your outputs from your "sandbox" in the right place in the developmental repository. This action is the opposite of the GET action.
CONDUCT: Also a great SPM "hook," this makes sure you get connected to the correct how-to methodology and roles for this important gate meeting. Only used in gate activities.

INSPECT: This is a critical hook to get to the inspection procedure. The described model has a heavy emphasis on detecting and correcting early defects. You want to drastically reduce test-time defects by attacking these possible defects earlier. The described model also has a heavy emphasis on placing "the monkey" on the producer's back — not the consumer's! I have worked for several companies where work products were handed off to the next person in line with a "good luck to you" attitude. Because this shows up in all activities, you need an efficient inspection procedure.

END: The purpose of this great SPM hook is to:

- Let key players know that this task is done. Key player could be:
  - The software project manager
  - The development manager
  - The development lead
  - The folks collecting earned value
  - Quality — in case they want to do near-real-time process audits
  - SCM (for repository management)
  - Accounting (for additional charge numbers)
- Pass off metrics data collection to the folks collecting this data

I have very effectively used a Web-based interface for these common high-level steps. I am going to discuss at length the role that the charge number has to this process model approach, and why you should seriously consider aligning charge numbers with process activities. At this point, I will merely say that if you could enter the charge number to this Web page interface, you could certainly derive the following dynamic information at execution time:

- The project you're working on
- The type of activity being executed
- The specific activity object being acted upon
- Whether this is an original or a reworked task
- Sufficiency of the information to know exactly what task we're talking about on your project schedule

The power of this dynamic information is enormous. Essentially, these common Web-based interfaces convert the static world of the activity to the dynamic world of the project schedule's task. It doesn't take too much imagination for you to have an ATM-like interface here, where you feed back something on the lines of "Are you on <Project XXX> using activity type <Activity Name> for object <object name>?" for a yes/no verification. With this information, you can easily tailor automatic e-mails to specific role responsibilities by project to streamline this activity-based communication. I leave it to you whether or not you take advantage of this awesome project role interface. Any of your hotshot programmers or Web master can easily do this.

Furthermore, when you add the filename, you know exactly which work product you're talking about for that particular task identified in previous paragraphs. This is a powerful capability to exactly extract inputs from the correct place in the SCM repository and place outputs in the correct place as well. You totally eliminate errors (and extra time) in controlling your developmental work products via this mechanism. The developers can be totally insulated from SCM controls to concentrate on their computer science reason-for-being.

The software engineers will love it — along with SCM and SPM. Also, inspections know exactly what specific work product is the target for inspection purposes. This can be captured for metrics purposes.

The GET, PUT, and INSPECT "hooks" all pass the filename to this Web interface in addition to the charge number. The INSPECT hook uses this mechanism to specifically identify where we are in the life cycle when the inspection occurs for a particular file. That is powerful information to store in our inspection database. GET and PUT are important SCM hooks and do considerably more behind the scenes for your developers. Let's look at these SCM interfaces separately.

I need to introduce the concept of a "sandbox" when talking about the GET and PUT "hooks." That's the common working area in which developmental repository files are placed (GET) and taken from (PUT) while an activity is executed. I will be talking more about this in Chapters 6 and 9. If you have a filename, the SCM procedure can retrieve this file from the correct place in the developmental repository (including the right version) for activity execution and do the reverse for outputs. This is shown graphically in Figure 5.6.

In this figure, the developmental repository is:

■ Activity object based (system pieces/parts) for its structure
■ Incrementally developed by SCM and triggered by END steps from the "Design Down" activity executions
■ Version controlled
■ Subject to any file "checked-out" being considered a read-only operation

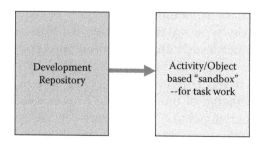

Figure 5.6   GET action.

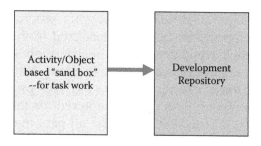

Figure 5.7   PUT action.

The sandbox is:

- Version controlled
- Activity based, statically
- Providing additional activity objects when known by SCM
- Incrementally developed by SCM and triggered by any END step from a "Design Down" activity execution
- So used as to ensure that any file checked into it (the sandbox) is for activity execution

A similar but opposite action occurs with the PUT operation. This is shown in Figure 5.7.

Of all the high-level steps, the INSPECT step needs special attention. It is the major hook to the inspection procedure. In this process model, I insist that each and every work product that should be inspected has a quality-inspection checklist associated with that work product. There should be a 1:1 correspondence of work products to inspection checklists. This is depicted in Figure 5.8.

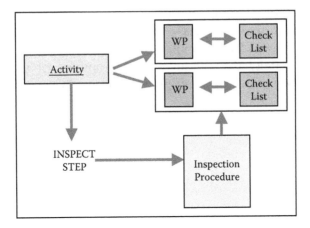

Figure 5.8   INSPECT action.

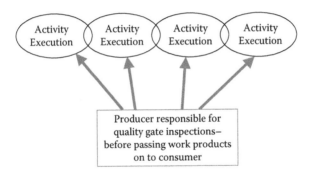

Figure 5.9   Life cycle as an inspection chain.

With inspections in place in each activity, you get inspections in place throughout your life cycle. This directly addresses the lower costs of detecting defects sooner rather than later — a boon to any software project manager. This link-chain effect is shown in Figure 5.9.

- Developers know what how-to procedures to use on this project.
- SQA knows what process elements are to be audited for this project.
- Subcontractors know what they need as how-to alternatives for scheduled activities.
- Customers know what processes you are using on their project.

It gets rid of all uncertainty when executing any project. Any software project manager has a vested interest in this. Additionally, your entire organization gets into the habit of refocusing attention on the process activity throughout the development of your schedule. How's that for really getting institutionalization of your processes on a culture fast track?

Chapter 6

Special Process Activities for Software Project Management

Introduction

I have established that in this process approach, there is a direct connection from process activities to project schedules. When we place activity instances on a project schedule, they become schedule tasks. The statically defined common steps within each activity can be used dynamically to tie procedural actions to a particular task in your project schedule. Furthermore, plans produced as a result of task execution can be directly applied by the software project manager to schedule planning. I intend to use process execution to not only progress toward a target system, but also to be heavily used by project managers to help with their software project management (SPM) effort.

There are two activities that have special interest to any software project manager:

- The "Design Down" activity
- The "Update Integration Plan" activity

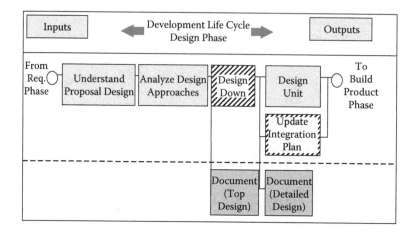

Figure 6.1 Possible "Design Phase" pad showing "Design Down" and "Update Integration Plan."

Figure 6.1 shows a possible design-phase-based process activity diagram (PAD) that includes these activities.

I will revisit this same PAD when I talk about project planning using an example scenario. I have purposely shaded the two activities in question to help you identify where they are inside this PAD. An astute reader may ask, "Why isn't the integration plan updated as part of the 'Design Down' activity?" After all, when you do top-level designs, you get more visibility on the lower-level pieces/parts of the system, right? The answer is that not all "Design Down" activity executions get an "Update Integration Plan" activity connected to them. Throughout this book, I have used "system" as the top level, "subsystem" as the next level, and "unit" as the lowest level. You may use terms different from these. You'll notice that by using the term "Design Down," I am not locked into any piece/part terminology at all. Most people recognize "Design Down" as a top-level design versus a detailed design type of activity. A "Design Down (system)" decomposes the design into subsystems. At this level, you don't have enough information to do any kind of integration planning. However, when you do "Design Down (subsystem)" executions that take you down to units, you have enough information to execute an "Update Integration Plan" activity.

The execution of the END step in these activities has a very special meaning to a software project manager. These particular END executions involve major players as follows:

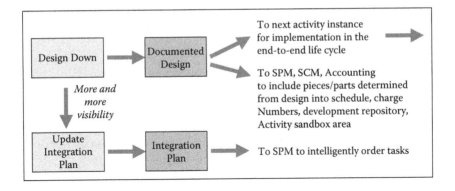

Figure 6.2   Impact of the two key SPM activities.

- Software configuration management (SCM; developmental repository actions)
- Accounting (charge number actions)
- Yourself as software project manager (schedule task planning and schedule task ordering)

As soon as your engineering design team identifies the lower-level pieces/parts, the project management partners can, in almost real-time, use that design for SCM controls, charge number expansion, and schedule task planning and ordering. This is a veritable n-for-one sale where engineering itself becomes a key SPM driver. With this method, engineering can no longer take a separate position from SPM. Engineering and SPM are now tightly bound via this process approach. The impact of these two activities is graphically shown in Figure 6.2.

SCM Actions

SCM has two distinct areas involved with the END step from any "Design Down" activity. These are:

- The evolving version-controlled software development repository
- The creation of "sandboxes" for any activity's internal work

A software project manager has a vital and vested interest in getting these done right and done timely — because it saves time.

At project start, SCM creates a skeleton developmental repository that has:

- A root project node
- A subfolder for proposal work products
- A subfolder for the system

At proposal time, SCM also populates this repository with known templates and placeholder files for any/all work products needed at proposal time. These become version 0 of the files.

At start-up time (front of execution), SCM adds all the work products and placeholders under the "System" node that are known at that system level. As in the previous paragraph, these become version 0 of these files. These populated files include templates or placeholders of all the known deliverables prepositioned in the correct place in that repository. At this point, SCM has no idea what the subsystem story is about this system because top-level design has not been done yet — so no further subfolders are created under the system node.

Now we get to the END SCM action on the "Design Down (system)" activity instance (or schedule task). At this time, SCM does know:

- The exact number of subsystems as per engineering design
- The exact name of those subsystems as per engineering design

SCM now creates a subfolder under "System" for each subsystem and names them according to the design. Also, SCM populates each subfolder with all the known file templates and placeholders for subsystem-related work products. As with the others, these become version 0 of these files. This is graphically shown in Figure 6.3.

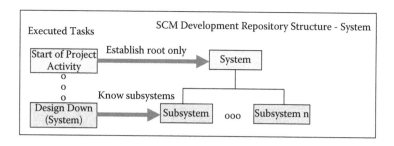

Figure 6.3 Allocating subsystem folders to the development repository.

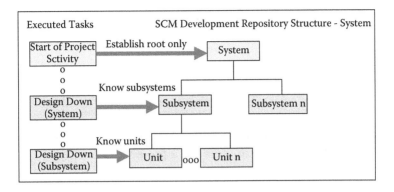

Figure 6.4   SCM repository expansion when units are known.

At this point, some readers are going to say, "We don't use SCM for this type of thing." In this process-based SPM approach, you use SCM directly to aid you in performing your work as a software project manager. If some of you are also questioning how SCM knows about work product templates, etc. — remember that tasks = activities = associated work products. The process will tell you this.

The same kind of thing happens when SCM gets notification of the END for any given subsystem. At this time SCM does know:

- The exact number of units within that subsystem as per engineering design
- The exact name of those units as per engineering design

SCM now creates a subfolder under the appropriate subsystem folder for each unit and names them according to the design. Also, SCM populates each subfolder with all the known file templates and placeholders for unit-related work products. As with the others, these become version 0 of these files. This is shown graphically in Figure 6.4.

In addition to expanding the developmental repository that is totally aligned with engineering design, SCM has an added role related to all the working "sandboxes" needed for development. By having these as SCM responsibilities, you remove all the "gotchas" with developers storing work products on their own C drive or desk drawer, etc. You also ensure that developers are versioning their work products even within their respective sandboxes. Any software project manager has got to be concerned about things such as developers getting sick, going on vacation, getting transferred, quitting, or even having accidents, etc.

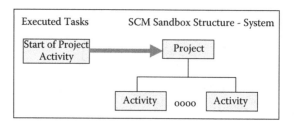

Figure 6.5   Initial sandbox structure for a project.

You have a high probability of recovering when SCM has control and responsibilities over these areas. From a personal experience, software engineers like it too, because it gets rid of all the dreary aspects of their job so that they can concentrate on programming (which they love). Also, this mechanism is identical from project to project. There is no learning curve involved with your development staff.

Let's turn our attention now to sandboxes set up by SCM. These are storage areas used by the assigned team members for any given schedule task. You want to set up a structure that has a virtual firewall around each and every sandbox so that interactivity interference does not occur. Again, we want to pay attention to data integrity to eliminate this from biting the software project manager.

Sandboxes are set up for each project as part of project setup at start of execution. SCM creates a root node for the designated project and a set of subfolders — one per activity name. We don't need a system subfolder, because the project root node serves both the project and system to be produced. This is shown in Figure 6.5.

Because generic objects are statically associated with process activities, we can relate execution-time-specific piece/part names to those generic names. "Design Unit" activity, for example, has a valid piece/part of a unit name as an activity object. As each "Design Down" activity is executed, we now know the decomposed piece/part from that design. A "Design Down (system)" execution provides SCM with real piece/part names of all the subsystems. These subsystem names become subfolders under those activities that allow that name. At this point, under the "Design Down" subfolder within the sandbox, you'd have a subfolder for each of the subsystems named from design. For each executed "Design Down (subsystem)," you'd know all the named units. SCM would create a subfolder for each and every named unit under those activities that allow unit names. Similarly, at this point, under the "Design Unit" subfolder within the sandbox, you'd have a

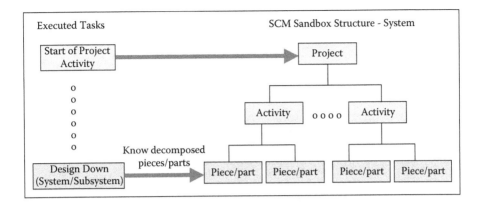

Figure 6.6   Sandbox areas elaborated as pieces/parts known.

subfolder for each of the units named from design. You'd also see the same lineup under "Implement Unit." This is shown in Figure 6.6.

What you end up with is a working (and version-controlled) area for each activity type/activity object combination for use by your developer during schedule execution. Each and every GET and PUT can intelligently store and retrieve work products from/to the developmental repository in separate work areas during schedule task executions. By doing this, you have significantly reduced/eliminated data conflicts and race conditions. The engineering staff know exactly where their sandbox is for activity execution-time processing. As software project manager, you are amply insulated from staffing hiccups and changes due to this mechanism.

Accounting Actions

Accounting has two actions involved with the END step from any "Design Down" activity. These are:

▪ Expand the project's charge number.
▪ Associate the new number with the symbolic piece/part name.

Just as previously observed, any END execution from a "Design Down" on your project schedule informs accounting that a top-level design is "done," and the appropriate level of pieces/parts have been identified and named. Armed with this information, accounting can now expand the activity-based charge numbers for your project to reflect the engineering design.

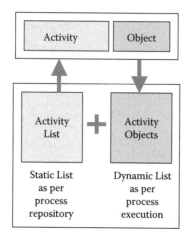

Figure 6.7 Schedulable part of a WBS.

At this point, you may be wondering how all this works because you already have a charge number system. I am advocating a charge number system that is totally aligned with processes and that makes it aligned to your schedule tasking. I fully understand that anyone suggesting a different charge number approach is probably going to be summarily tossed out the door. I hope to show you unbelievable benefits in aligning your charge numbers to process and schedules.

In my approach, I first of all tackle the work breakdown structure (WBS). I have divided the WBS format, in general, into two categories:

- To cover schedulable work
- To cover nonschedulable and other work

The general makeup of the former is shown in Figure 6.7. Later in the book (Chapters 12 and 14), I will take you through an example in which I show you how this gets elaborated and how it is aligned to the process activities and activity objects. These are the same entities that show up on project schedules for actual work.

The form for the latter is shown in Figure 6.8. These cover a host of other items and event-driven procedural work from the process model approach.

I am suggesting a charge numbering system that has your WBS embedded in it as shown in Figure 6.9.

This format essentially places the project ID as a prefix and rework counter as a suffix around the WBS. This charge number approach is made up of four general sections:

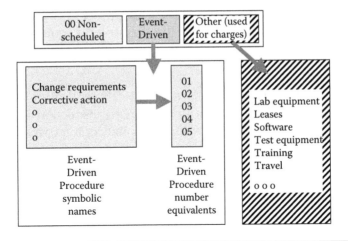

Figure 6.8 Nonschedulable portion of the WBS.

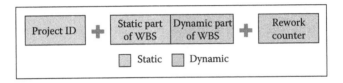

Figure 6.9 Time charging number breakdown.

- Project ID
- Static part of the WBS
- Dynamic part of the WBS
- Rework counter

It is the dynamic part that will be determined by engineering design and filled in by accounting. In the project-setup portion of this book (Chapter 12), I will describe a 9-digit format as an example.

Engineering Development Actions

In this process-based SPM approach, I do suggest the following actions from engineering development when executing any "Design Down" and "Update Integration Plan." Many companies are not currently doing this.

"Design Down (subsystem)" activity executions: For those top-level designs that decompose down to the unit level, I require:

- The exact number of units and their unique names
- Whether the units:
  - Need coding with unit test (typically critical units)
  - Need coding without unit test (i.e., inspection is sufficient)
  - Are reused units but still need some coding (tweaking) along with unit test
  - Are reused units but still need some coding (tweaking) with no unit test
  - Are reused units we can use as is
- Units that need to be done early (even before we do any integration planning)

The first bulleted item is critical for SCM, SPM, and accounting. The last two bulleted items are extremely useful to an SPM and will significantly reduce or eliminate schedule rework. Information about each unit totally corresponds to activity selectability on a project schedule. That's why we need this information. Engineering development really does know up front which units are of higher priorities than others for execution — even prior to integration planning. This information allows the software project manager to lay out the execution of those units on the schedule before the integration plan is finished. It is really the integration plan that gives the software project manager insight into execution ordering. In the meantime, the software project manager can intelligently place unit executions on a schedule, based on engineering input. I realize this is a little more than most designs do — but this information is absolutely necessary for a software project manager in this approach.

"Update Integration Plan" activity executions: For these activities, I require:

- Units to be grouped into integration sets that go together for integration
- Each integration set to be named with its units identified
- Integration ordering by integration set

Integration sets can span subsystems. As a result of the integration planning done by engineering development, the software project manager can now flesh out the remainder of the schedule under the direction of that plan. The software project manager can delay some units while moving up others for just-in-time integrations. Furthermore, if your company flows requirements down to the integration sets specified in the integration plan, qualified system testing can be started immediately after integration executions. This can really shorten up the time-to-market schedule. I talk a lot more about this in Chapter 14.

SPM Actions

After every "Design Down" END notification, the software project manager will know:

- The exact decomposed design pieces/parts and their names
- Whether any "Implement Code" activity gets placed on the schedule for any given unit
- Whether any "Test Unit" activity gets placed on the schedule for any given unit — along with the "Create Unit Test" activity to create the unit driver
- Those activities that are totally reused and off-the-shelf
- Those units that are known to be early contenders for schedule planning

In other words, the software project manager has the complete piece/part schedule identification story. The software project manager also knows what subset of that story can be placed on the schedule, with a high certainty that it stays put (i.e., no rework). What the software project manager does not know is the ordering of the rest of that story. That information is provided when the integration plan is implemented.

After every "Update Integration Plan" END notification, the software project manager will know:

- The number of integration sets
- The number of "integrate" executions
- The unit execution ordering for the rest of the piece/part story

As I mentioned earlier, the software project manager can do intelligent early (but qualified) system testing directly tied in with the termination of each "Integrate" — if requirements were flowed down to these integration sets. The software project manager should be able to completely map out the project schedule with this information from engineering development. This makes engineering a real role partner with the software project manager for project success.

INSTITUTIONAL-IZATION CONSIDERATIONS

Chapter 7

Process Framework Model Institutionalized

Introduction

To be really effective in performing software project management (SPM) using this process-based approach, you need the entire process environment to be an integral part of everyone's day-to-day life. To reach that goal, the process model has to be an active part of your company culture.

Let's start with the process framework architectural model itself. At this point, I'm really talking to many companies out there who have piles of processes that have these characteristics:

- Paper based in binders
- Mix and match of policies, what you need to do, and how you need to do it
- No relationship of process elements to your project schedules
- No relationship of process elements to your project life cycles
- Verbosity
- Pretty looks only (nice graphic glossies)
- Little to no active use

If I have described your company's situation, you probably have a useless pile of stuff that no one uses or cares about. You have probably spent a lot of money developing this useless pile. Believe it or not, these companies would rather stay with this than change. They are quite willing to continue with poor quality, no repeatability, chaos, fire fighting, and high costs until the end of the company itself. I mention this because I have experienced that very situation. A process guy such as me would be considered the enemy rather than a supporting person. Making my proposed changes will have incredible benefits.

The process architectural model approach I'm describing is organized with a place for everything, but can also be just "nice" if not institutionalized. The big thing I've learned over the years is that practitioners and managers alike will use your processes if, among other things, they:

- Make sense
- Are short and to the point
- Aid (not hinder) them in their jobs
- Don't insult their intelligence
- Aren't overbearing

With this approach, the processes need to be a "click" away and need to be totally integrated into everything.

Process Repository Institutionalized

The first order of business is the process repository itself. This needs to be a Web-based, version-controlled repository. I have personally used two products for this very thing:

- LiveLink
- SharePoint

I am not endorsing these products. I understand there are more candidates out there — except that I have had experience only with these two applications. Unfortunately, there are many companies who still cling to the notion of a process repository as one area and a Web repository as another area. You can do this, but why? You are asking for trouble by maintaining two separate repositories and keeping them in sync for changes. It's so much easier to have one and only one repository that has a dual function:

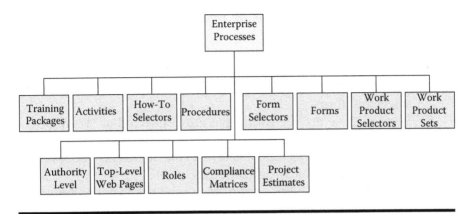

Figure 7.1   Process repository structure.

- Keeping different versions of all your process elements
- Automatically using the latest version (tip) for intranet Web displays and access

Versioning is vital, particularly for process elements. When you start up any project, you have a single piece of information that is critical for determining your process basis — the project start date. With that date, you can automatically determine all the process elements that are candidates for your project. I will describe this later in this chapter. As time goes on, processes change. No software project manager wants to automatically chase the process "tail" for process improvements. Chasing process improvements can cause disruptions in your project. If you're at a point in the life cycle when you can step up to a later version of a process element, this should be your choice. By having the Web-displayed version as the latest and greatest process version, there is a built-in incentive to stay current for any software project manager — without forcing a step up to that version.

Figure 7.1 shows a process repository structure that I have used.

You'll notice a very flat structure. The names of the subfolders are the same names in the two-row table shown at the top of Figure 4.3 through Figure 4.6, except for "Top-Level Web Pages." Every Web page has a hyperlink reference to all these subfolders for rapid access to process elements. The process repository is subdivided into these subfolders:

1. Activities. These are the "What you have to do" process elements that are portrayed inside process activity diagrams (PADs) and show up as schedule tasks.

2. How-To Selectors. These are the front-end process elements to selectable how-to procedures.
3. Procedures. These are the "How you are to do it" process elements that are connected to "How-To Selectors."
4. Form Selectors. These are the front-end process elements to selectable forms.
5. Forms. These are the forms that are connected to "Form Selectors."
6. Work Product Selectors. These are the front-end process elements to selectable work products.
7. Work Products. These are the work products that are connected to "Work Product Selectors."
8. Roles. This is where all described roles are located. Any role-reference hyperlinks into this file at the appropriate anchor point.
9. Training Packages. This is where all the training packages exist, which are mentioned with activities or procedures.
10. Project Estimates. This is where you retain companywide estimation data to help any SPM.
11. Authority Level. These are where all the high-level requirements are kept or referenced, and they include ISO 9001, CMMI, regulations, and company policies.
12. Compliance Matrices. This is where you have all the process compliance tracing to authority-level standards, maturity models, or policies.
13. Top-Level Web Pages. This is self-explanatory.

Of these 13 items, the first 12 should show up on all Web pages for direct connectivity to these areas. All use the last item implicitly as they use the Web. Of these same 13 items, practitioners and management primarily use the first 10. The last 3 items tend to be of more interest to your software engineering process group (SEPG), assessors, or auditors. The beauty of direct hyperlinking into this process repository is that you get a list of files automatically arranged in alphabetical order. On file access, you automatically get the latest version.

Within each subfolder, you should have versions of each and every file. This is shown graphically in Figure 7.2.

As part of institutionalization, I highly recommend that every process element inside the process repository use a date only as a version. I further recommend that the date be in the YYYYMMDD format. There are some very good reasons behind this:

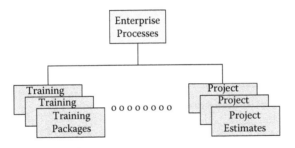

Figure 7.2 Each category version-controlled.

- Revision numbers are too cumbersome. For process elements, you want to encourage updates for process improvements without going through the Arabic numbering system.
- Revision letters make no sense at all for process elements. You can get into the A … Z, AA … ZZ, AAA … ZZZ mode really fast.
- The YYYYMMDD form can be easily compared to any project start date to determine a process basis via script processing. Dates "equal to" or closest "less than" the project start date are the candidate process basis set. Make it easy on yourself.
- Version date can be an HTML tag. HTML ignores tags that it doesn't recognize. You can easily add something such as <Process-Version> YYYYMMDD </Process-Version> in your HTML file for script processing.

I know this defies conventional wisdom for version identification, but I hope you can see why this will simplify your institutionalized processes.

With a version-controlled process repository, we now have an incredibly simple way of performing process updates. This is shown in Figure 7.3.

In most companies, the SEPG will be the group that actually makes changes to process elements. Because we are dealing with a version-controlled repository, we "Checkout-for-Update" the file that we want to change and make necessary changes to the checked out file. As you can see from the flowchart, if the changes are trivial, typos, or minor in nature, it is just fine to do a "Check in" back into the repository. This action automatically makes it "live" for Web access. If the changes are considered substantive, I recommend an inspection on the changes before doing that "Check in" operation. This change procedure works well with single-process elements or multiple-associative elements.

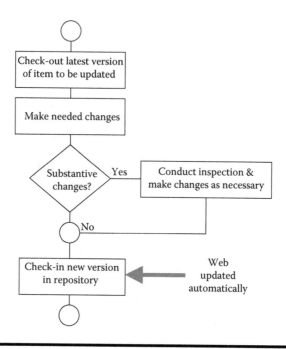

Figure 7.3   Simple process update procedure.

Script Programming Institutionalized

I really believe that you can create some awesome metrics automatically for your process repository with some fairly simple script programming.

To support script programming, you need to embed HTML tags within your process elements. As I've stated before, HTML has a characteristic that is absolutely great for process elements — it ignores tags it doesn't recognize. This opens the door for your SEPG to embed process-related HTML tags in each and every process element that is ignored by HTML but used by your script programming.

This process model approach is role based for activities, procedures, work products, and forms. Wouldn't it be great to know the following:

- What is the major ownership role for any process element?
- What roles show up where — throughout the process repository?
- Who "owns" certain work products?
- Who "owns" certain forms?
- What roles are associated with what training package?

```
ooo
ooo
<ProcessRoles>
    SQA,
    SCA,
    Software Engineer
</ProcessRoles>
ooo
ooo
```

Figure 7.4 HTML tag example for script processing.

Roles	Process Activities					
SQA						X
SCM			X		X	
SW Engineer		X	X	X		
Etc.						

Figure 7.5 Sample script output — role involvements.

Just think about employee training for a minute. If you have an SCM analyst, you could identify all the SCM process elements that "belong" to SCM. In addition, you could identify where SCM shows up throughout any/all process elements. This is no longer a guess — but accurate. Figure 7.4 shows an example of embedded HTML tags. The only rule that your SEPG has to follow is that embedded process-related tags follow HTML rules.

With a little bit more script programming, you could easily generate a matrix showing activities (or procedures) along one side and roles down the other. Whenever that role is involved in that process element, an "X" is placed at the intersection of these two items. This is shown in Figure 7.5. These kinds of matrices provide a top-level view of role participation throughout your processes. I hope the reader will readily

Roles	Work Products				
SQA			X		X	
SCM		X				
SW Engineer		X	X	X		
Etc.						

Figure 7.6   Sample script output roles and work products.

see that software project managers or development managers can use this for task resource allocations. You can also use this as a functional area training guide. This can be used for new hire or transfer personnel training as well. You get all this via institutionalized script programming.

In the process world, another big question involves the relationship of roles to work products. This can also be achieved with script programming, using the embedded process-oriented HTML tags. Figure 7.6 shows a similar matrix as before, except that roles are mapped to work products. Do something similar for forms.

In the training world, you don't build training packages in a vacuum. You build them for a specific purpose and for specific roles. With this process-based SPM approach, we explicitly identify training requirements within pertinent activities and procedures. Both activities and procedures identify roles involved in those process elements. With institutionalized script programming, you can easily map your training packages to where they are needed within your process elements. This is shown in Figure 7.7.

Inspection Procedure Institutionalized

From an institutionalized perspective, inspections have two major components that need to be addressed at the company level:

- The inspection procedure itself
- Inspection checklists — one per work product that requires an inspection

Training Packages	Process Elements					
Framework	X	X	X	X	X	X
Requirements	X					
Inspection Procedure	X	X	X	X	X	
Etc.						

Figure 7.7   Sample script output for training packages.

Many companies may have the former and not the latter. For these companies, something is thrown on your desk with a "check this" type of command. It's no wonder that people waste a lot of time in this environment over spelling, typos, styles, etc. — all of which are in the noise level and don't produce quality inspections. That's why inspections have a bad name.

The most important procedure in this process-based SPM approach is the inspection procedure. Some companies call them *reviews* (in error, according to me). If you don't have one, you need one. If you do have one, is it efficient? Is it used? Is its use haphazard? Can it support multisite inspections? Can it support both defect detection and prevention? I have personally seen awful examples of inspection procedures. I have been at more than one company that has certainly had an inspection (or review) procedure that was so bad that no one used it. One company had so many bells and whistles built in for metrics purposes that people dreaded the experience of using it at all. Don't do this, especially when you're not a mature organization and people are not even paper trained on process! I am a big proponent of keeping it simple. People will use an inspection procedure if they see value to it. They won't if they see no value to it or consider it a waste of time. The absolutely worst one I saw with document inspections was done by making transparencies of each and every page of the document, inviting 20 people into a room, and then flipping through the transparencies using an overhead projector. The inspection was done page by page. The moderator asked questions such as, "Does anyone have anything on page 1?" These inspections took a long time and ended up finding things such as missing semicolons, spacing issues, bullets versus numbers, and all kinds of petty things. People hated to show up at these inspections because it shot down a good chunk of the day. If you have that kind of inspection, I feel sorry for you.

As an aside and being a process purist, I really mean "inspection" and not "review." I make a huge distinction between these two terms. The primary purpose of an inspection is to find (and fix) defects. The primary purpose of a review is to externalize one or more work products to your audience, with a side possibility of finding defects. The focus is different in these two definitions. I want inspections. In the DoD contracting world, you see major reviews called out, in which large numbers of people are gathered in a room to go over top-level or detailed designs. This use of "review" really does externalize those designs to the gathered group and, yes, they sometimes find defects! Finding defects is not the main purpose of them being there.

Let me refer you back to Figure 5.8 to put this inspection procedure in context. You get to the inspection procedure via the INSPECT step within activities. In this process model, INSPECT is hyperlinked to the INSPECT How-To Selector, which, in turn, gets you to the inspection procedure. The How-To Selector is important inasmuch as you can have more than one inspection procedure to select. I found this very useful for:

- Allowing a new inspection procedure to be introduced
- Allowing inspection procedure variations across groups/sites/countries
- Allowing for scalable inspection procedures based on type of project

Trying to introduce a better inspection "mousetrap" at many companies is very difficult, especially when the old version is somebody's "baby." I have been shot down more than once over this very thing. The beauty of an INSPECT How-To Selector is that you can introduce a new and better approach while leaving the old one there. A simple Web counter really helps here. If, over time, you have 1000 hits on one form of inspection procedure versus 10 hits on another, it's a really good indicator of which one should be kept and which one should be dropped. Numbers don't lie.

A basic inspection procedure should:

- Be intranet based for maximum inspection value.
- Have inspection roles defined (e.g., author, inspector, and work product lead).

- Take inspection direction from an inspection checklist. Checklist is subdivided by inspection criteria, by role, and by author's entry criteria for that inspection.
- Create findings based on defects, summarizing "noise" defects.
- Minimize elapsed time between individual inspections and inspection meeting.
- Support offline author responses to inspector findings, to minimize inspection meeting time.
- Use prioritized findings as the inspection meeting agenda.
- Support defect prevention, i.e., where defect should have been picked up.

In this process model, INSPECT passes the charge number and filename from any given task execution to the inspection procedure. This provides the inspection procedure with the following derived information:

- The project involved
- The activity type involved
- The activity object involved for that activity type
- Data on whether this was an inspection involved with rework

The filename provides the inspection procedure with the exact target file ID of the file or work product being inspected. Inspections, by definition, are conducted against files in the activity's sandbox area. So, the inspection procedure knows exactly which part of the sandbox is involved, and which file within that sandbox is the target file. There is absolutely no ambiguity with any inspection because of this process model.

With this process model approach, you know where you are in any project. You know where defects have been found. These get deduced directly from the charge number parameter. If your inspectors think any defect should have been found earlier in the life cycle, they can either select an activity name from a drop-down list of activity names to provide the appropriate defect prevention capability or just indicate this finding as a "Defect Prevention" one for the SEPG to determine. Your SEPG can take this information and improve an earlier checklist to address that defect. How's that for a closed-loop process improvement method?

At this point, any traditional software project manager will probably be saying, "That's all very nice, but what has that got to do with SPM?" As a software project manager, you want defects caught early because it's cheaper and it doesn't create defect compounding throughout the project. You really want to head toward a smooth (almost uneventful) system test position. That's why I have emphasized the importance of an efficient inspection procedure for SPM. You want the monkey on the producer's back for quality. I have to admit that just having inspections improves quality. If I were a developer and I knew that my internal work product was going to be scrutinized by my peers, you better believe that I will get that item in as good a shape as possible before any inspection. I just don't want to look bad in front of my colleagues.

Inspection Checklists Institutionalized

The other big point to observe in the referenced Figure 5.8 is that each work product has its own inspection checklist. I cringe when I see inspection checklists hung off the inspection procedure. The checklist needs to go with the targeted work product. They are a matched set.

Figure 7.8 shows an inspection checklist format that I found to be very effective.

In the top portion of the checklist, place the suggested inspector roles involved in this inspection. That information is a great help to the work product lead who is calling for the inspection. I have found that inviting your internal customer as an inspector is very useful to

Figure 7.8 Basic inspection checklist.

improve quality. As an aside, if the author thinks the consumer of his or her efforts is an inspector, you'll be amazed at the higher degree of quality reached before the inspection.

The body of the inspection checklist is subdivided into three major chunks:

- Author Entry Criteria
- Inspection Criteria (Technical Role)
- Inspection Criteria (Nontechnical Role)

For the author entry criteria, this is a great place to put all the mind-jogger items that you want the author to do prior to the inspection.

If the inspected work product were a document, you'd see, among others, author mind-jogger things such as:

- Has document been spell-checked?
- Has table of contents been updated correctly?
- Is pagination correct?
- Are document headers correct?

If the inspected work product were coded in C++, you'd see, among others, author mind-jogger things such as:

- Has lint been run (or equivalent)?
- Is code header correct?
- Were coding guidelines followed?

Finally, you take all the inspection questions and organize them into at least two categories: technical and nontechnical. It is insane to have a technical person spend time inspecting nontechnical parts of a work product. Use them wisely and have them inspect areas that they know. Conversely, have nontechnical people inspect the nontechnical aspects of work products. Technical editors do a marvelous job at style/format types of things, for example. Software programmers are horrible in that role. In my experience, software programmers are definitely not English majors. Grammar and sentences are not their bag. Any misalignment here can cost the software project manager a lot in wasted productivity, time, and slipped schedules.

This is why you need the concept of inspection checklists connected to work products that, in turn, are used by the inspection procedure to be institutionalized.

Activity Estimations Institutionalized

One of the standard attributes in all activities is "Activity estimates." This was originally shown in Figure 5.3 when I showed what an activity would look as a Web page. What exactly does that mean?

The very essence of estimation is to divide and conquer. You take the whole effort and keep breaking it down into manageable chunks. The idea is that estimation variances on any given manageable chunk should be close to reality when you finally get around to executing that chunk. You finally map out the chunk pieces to reflect possible concurrent operations and predecessor/successor relationships as a complete roadmap back up to the entire job at hand. That's what estimation is all about. The end resultant estimation is comprised of smaller estimations that feed into the final estimation.

After doing that drill, you need to add a loading factor to allow for vacations, sick time, and overhead support functions, which are real but don't show up when estimating target systems. Clearly, if your engineering staff were senior people with 4 to 6 weeks vacations, that loading factor would be very different than if your staff had 2 weeks vacation. If you were programming in downtown Baghdad versus downtown Cleveland, the loading factor would need to include massive security overhead costs. I will now show you why this process approach really simplifies the estimation effort by attaching a loading factor to each and every activity rather than a global loading factor approach. This granularity will provide a more accurate estimation approach.

Because process activities become schedule tasks, the entire project schedule can be subdivided into activity types. Furthermore, when charge numbers are aligned to activities, you can extract real-world costs in manpower and durations for all activities or tasks in a schedule. These actuals provide the input grist for future estimations. For the first time up — no prior actuals for estimation — you really do need to provide an educated guess for each activity type and keep your fingers crossed.

With this actual data extracted from your project schedule execution, I am suggesting that you do some simple things such as:

■ Taking an actual average estimate (dollars, duration, manpower, etc.) for each activity type. If you had 200 "Implement Unit" activities in a project schedule, I maintain that you can rapidly determine what an average "Implement Unit" means. Also, you are not restricted to a single project. You can get better and better estimates over multiple projects that, over time, will improve progressively. For low-usage activities such as "Design Down," you may need multiple projects to get a more accurate average estimation.

■ Taking an actual MIN estimate. I am not a statistical person, but wiser heads than mine can take a set of real-world actuals and determine a minimum value or values for estimation purposes. Statistically, you would discard deviations from the norm.

■ Taking an actual MAX estimate. Just as earlier, take a set of real-world actuals and determine a maximum value or values for estimation purposes. Statistically, you would discard deviations from the norm.

Unlike the traditional way of estimating, I would then take each activity's AVG estimation data and add your loading factor to the activity's average estimations. Typically, loading factors are expressed as a percentage. This provides an average for estimation purposes to be used by the software project manager. I have called this estimation the L-AVG for loaded average. You can call it what you want. When going through an estimation breakdown drill, the software project manager uses:

■ The AVG for all pre-execution activities to be worked. The straight average is used because all this work is nonpaid and is part of your overhead-loading factor.

■ The L-AVG for all execution activities to be worked. The loaded average is used because you want to include the overhead factor.

To summarize, each activity type will have four estimation sets of values:

■ MIN (low need)
■ AVG (basis for L-AVG calculation and used for pre-execution activity work)
■ MAX (earned value variance trigger)
■ L-AVG (used for activity estimates at execution time by the SPM)

Of these, the software project manager will be using the last two items:

- When tracking, actuals exceeding the activity's MAX will trigger a variance report as part of any earned value system. Actuals within the MIN to MAX range are to be considered OK. This provides reasonable wiggle room for your development staff.
- L-AVG is used per execution-time activity and rolled up for each activity group if you want to create planning packages. The activity group becomes your planning package; e.g., the "design" activity group is made up of activities such as:
  - "Determine Design Approach"
  - "Design Down"
  - "Design Unit"

All these estimations are attached to each activity and updated after each project closes down. I do realize that you may have more than one set of four things if you have multiple life cycles in which activity actuals are widely different from one life cycle to the other. That's your call for this capability.

I suggest you make these four values available via the "Activity estimates" hyperlink within each activity. You may certainly add other supporting information such as experience levels of the people behind these estimates, etc.

The point is that activities and tasks are one and the same thing. Charge numbers are aligned to activities, and thus to tasks. Actuals come directly out of your time card system. Those same actuals have a feedback loop for new estimations. This is one area in which data from the time card system is crunched and made available to the activity process elements for further estimations. This whole aspect of estimation needs to be institutionalized.

Chapter 8

Work Breakdown Structure and Charge Numbers Institutionalized

Introduction

This is one area that, if done correctly, will yield enormous benefits. There will be readers for whom the work breakdown structure (WBS) or charge number system is so sacrosanct that it will take an act of Congress to change it. I hope to show you that by adopting the methodology described in this book, tremendous software project management (SPM) control is possible over your projects.

Before getting into this, I want to define *work* in this process-based SPM approach. I would like to see this WBS or charge number system invoked at the very beginning of the life cycle. You may have had several false starts in the business development area, but you would have surely expended costs and efforts in the pre-execution segment of any life cycle. Ideally, you should be able to capture all this and factor it into your loaded averages per activity. I will discuss this later on in this chapter. Pretending that work starts at the beginning of execution is crazy. Work starts before proposal time and continues after proposal time. With this process-based technique, we now have a really good way of capturing those work costs because all the pre-execution activities are uniquely named and associated with nonpaid work effort.

Let's look at a top-level view of WBS and charge numbers. Software costs money to create. These costs come from the following:

■ Actual work performed
■ Other things

All costs should be captured via a charge number in the time card system. You want to know if person A is performing design versus system test. If you were building a house, you would want to know foundation costs versus drywall costs. These kinds of costs reflect the work done. So, part of any charge number system should incorporate work-related costs versus nonwork-related costs. For example, buying software applications, "seats" for software usage, or plane tickets involve costs, but these are not work related.

The work-related charges are reflected in a WBS part of the charge number, whereas the nonwork-related charges are reflected in another part of the charge number. The bottom line is that both of these costs need a way of being organized so that it is meaningful to any person familiar with accounting.

Traditionally, most WBSs are based on piece/part or functional area. Using the house example, there would be structures that captured costs for the following:

■ Foundation
■ Framing
■ Roofing
■ Electrical
■ Plumbing

In this case, each of these areas usually calls for different skill sets.

WBS Institutionalized

In my process-based method, I will be using a nontraditional approach for the WBS that is process based. I maintain that you can achieve a piece/part view as well using a process perspective.

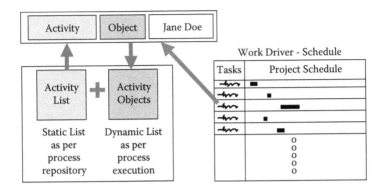

Figure 8.1 Schedulable perspective of a work breakdown structure (WBS).

I have already established the direct connection between process activities and schedule tasks. *Schedule tasks* are merely execution instances of one or more process activities. If you look back at Figure 4.7, you should notice that task items are made up of three main components:

- Activity name
- Activity object
- Activity lead

The first of these identifies the specific process activity being used. The second identifies the piece/part being acted on by that activity. The last element (the person) is the individual (along with all the employees) who are filling in the time charges.

I will now direct you to Figure 8.1.

This figure shows the connection of those first two schedule-tasking elements to the schedulable perspective of the WBS. I hope the reader will see that a number that comes directly from the activity list in the process repository can represent the activity itself. It is my opinion that an engineering development life cycle should have about 40 process activities for all schedule task instances. These activities can be assigned a unique activity number — usually a two-digit number. By this activity assignment, you can specifically identify work done by an activity type. For example, all executions of a "Design Down" activity provide you with work done for top-level design work. Similarly, all executions of an "Implement Unit" activity provide you with work done for coding development work.

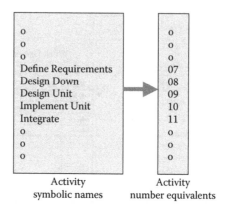

Figure 8.2   Symbolic activity name connection to the WBS number.

Let's turn our attention to the activity object in Figure 8.1. You will only know the piece/part story after you execute the "Design Down" activity. As I have mentioned earlier, the END step in that special activity triggers action by accounting to expand the dynamic part of the WBS (also wholly contained within a charge number) for all the newly designed pieces/parts. This really creates an indented parts list based on the design that is incorporated into the WBS and charge number system.

We now have tasks on a project schedule containing the symbolic names of the activity and activity object that are totally aligned with numbered equivalents in the WBS (and charge number). The activity part of the WBS is static. The activity object part of the WBS is dynamic. If you want a process view of the WBS, you will use the activity as your basis. If you want a piece/part view, you will use the activity object as your basis. The piece/part view does require that you include all activities that have the same activity object (or offshoots of that object).

Let's dig a little deeper and look into accounting's actions regarding the WBS and activities. All activities in the process repository get assigned a unique activity number. This action is shown in Figure 8.2.

I have shown a two-digit numbering scheme that should be sufficient for most companies. I have also numbered activities from 01 to 99, leaving out 00 for a reason. This provides a very flat structure for your WBS. If you want more of a hierarchy for your WBS, you could easily take it to the next level and incorporate activity groups into your WBS as well. I have shown this in Figure 8.3.

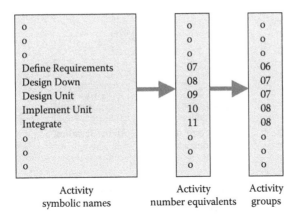

Figure 8.3   Can add WBS hierarchy via activity groups.

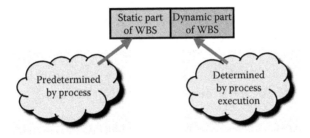

Figure 8.4   Top-level view of the WBS.

You'll notice that "Design Down" (or activity #08) and "Design Unit" (or activity #09) both belong to the "Design" activity group (#07). You could include the activity group number into your WBS if you really wanted a structure that was not flat. That, however, would take up four numbers versus two. I maintain you can always deduce activity groups without the additional two-digit number in your WBS. That's just me. You choose. Both activities and activity groups are static for accounting.

Let's now look at the WBS at a top level. This is depicted in Figure 8.4.

Essentially, you have a fixed part that is determined by process and a dynamic part determined by the pieces/parts as per design activity executions. Looking at the static part, we have already established that activities are numbered from 01 to 99. We now use 00 to make the top-level breakdown of a WBS, as in Figure 8.5.

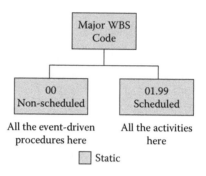

Figure 8.5   Top-level structure of the WBS.

I have broken the whole top-level WBS into two main camps as follows:

- The nonscheduled world as identified by the 00 code.
- The scheduled world as identified by the range 01 through 99 for all the activities in the process repository.

I found this to be a clean division of work at this level.
This process model deals with the following:

- Schedulable process elements, called *activities*
- Nonschedulable process elements, called *event-driven procedures*

Work occurs in both areas. The former type of work can be seen on the project schedule. The latter type of work cannot — but it still costs time and money. We need to allow for both of these in our WBS method.

Drilling down on the nonscheduled part of the WBS (signified by 00 at the root level), I have further subdivided that category as shown in Figure 8.6.

This figure shows that I have subdivided this nonscheduled world into two categories as follows:

- Other (depicted by another 00 code)
- Event-driven procedures numbered 01 to 99

At this point of the WBS numbering development, a front-end 0000 signifies "nonscheduled or other." A 00XX (where XX is a unique identifier for an event-driven procedure) signifies a nonscheduled

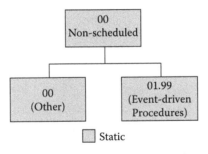

Figure 8.6   Nonscheduled part of the WBS.

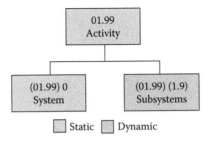

Figure 8.7   Scheduled part of the WBS.

procedure for work purposes. All information at this WBS development stage is static in nature. We can now capture work done on this project for all the invoked event-driven procedures that don't show up on the software project manager's schedule.

Let's look at the scheduled side of the WBS from the top down. This is shown in Figure 8.7.

Any leading two-digit number (in the range of 01 to 99) is, by definition, an activity type. In the system hierarchy I have used, the ordering is as follows:

- System
- Subsystem
- Unit

You may have other orders and nomenclature. Next, I assigned a single digit to the next layer as follows:

- 0 for system
- 1 to 9 for subsystems

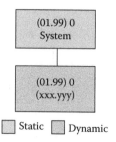

Figure 8.8   System part of the WBS.

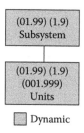

Figure 8.9   Subsystem or unit part of the WBS.

Clearly, if your business has a system with 15 subsystems, you'll need a two-digit number to express this. It is interesting to note here that the system part is static, whereas the subsystem part is dynamic — based on system design. This breakdown is shown in Figure 8.7.

For the system (0) WBS elements, I followed the 0 with a three-digit code for all the items that you want at the system level. If you have unique activity names in the pre-execution part of the life cycle versus those in the execution part of the life cycle, all the earlier target activities can all be associated at this system level. These are things such as deliverables, integration sets, etc. I chose not to add much more here. This breakdown is shown in Figure 8.8.

For any particular subsystem, these break down into units within that subsystem. The unit numbering is subsystem dependent, and I have represented units with a three-digit number per subsystem. Figure 8.9 shows this breakdown. Please note that this part of the WBS is dynamic — based on executed top-level designs.

So now, just looking at the first six digits of a WBS that had 041003, I can tell you that this is work related to the following:

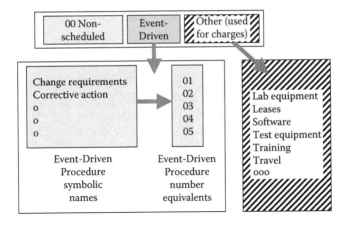

Figure 8.10   Nonscheduled and other perspective of the WBS.

- Activity #04
- Subsystem #1
- Unit #003 within subsystem #1

The subsystem part of this is a qualifier of the unit we're talking about. If activity #4 was an "Implement Unit" type of activity, then we're talking about work done using that activity on unit file abc.c (#003) within subsystem 1. That ties the WBS right to the task in the schedule that matches those parameters, namely, an "Implement Unit (abc.c)" task.

When it comes to the nonscheduled part of the WBS and "other" things, I am cheating a bit by including nonwork charge items within the WBS numbering system to conserve numbering space. For any purist, WBS numbers should only reflect work-related charges. Let me show you how I handled the "other" problem, shown in Figure 8.10.

I took the 00 leading two digits to represent "nonscheduled," followed by a two-digit number for event-driven procedures. I numbered event-driven procedures from 01 onward. I left the 00 designation to mean "other." Now, if there was a WBS with leading 0000 numbers, that opens the door for me to follow these zeros with a two-digit number for all the other (nonwork-related) things such as the following:

- Lab equipment
- Leases
- Software

- Test equipment
- Training
- Travel

You end up with a WBS that is a six-digit WBS number with different meanings based on scheduled versus nonscheduled; i.e.:

Scheduled:
  AA — Activities (01 ... 99)
  S —System (0) or subsystems (1 ... 9)
  UUU — System-related things or subsystem units (001 ... 999)
Nonscheduled:
  00 — Signifying nonscheduled
  PP — Other (00) or event-driven procedures (01 ... 99)
  MM — 00 for event-driven procedures or other miscellaneous
    items

Now we place the entire WBS inside the charge numbering scheme.

Charge Number Institutionalized

The charge number that people put on their time cards will now be as shown in Figure 8.11.

This charge number is subdivided into three big chunks as follows:

- Project ID
- WBS (static part and dynamic part)
- Rework counter

The project ID prefix is a unique number for your project. I have used a two-digit number here, reusing the numbers when I reached 99. We have just discussed the makeup of the WBS. The rework counter suffix is a single-digit number that reflects whether or not there is rework. I used the following:

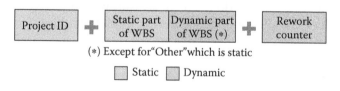

(∗) Except for "Other" which is static

☐ Static ☐ Dynamic

Figure 8.11   Time charging system.

- 0 for no rework; i.e., the original work
- 1 ... 9 for a rework counter, cycling around this range

Every activity instance placed on a project schedule gets a rework counter of 0 to represent original work. If the software project manager has to prune the schedule for things such as requirements changes and move schedule "branches" further down the schedule, these repeated (or reworked) tasks get a 1 suffix. If you ever get to reworking reworked activities, the counter goes to 2, etc.

This charge number system exactly aligns to this process-based SPM method, providing an incredible array of benefits, which include the following:

- Charge number matches schedule tasking for scheduled work.
- Charge number matches event-driven procedural work for all nonscheduled work.
- Charge number, when passed from common steps within any activity, makes the link from the static process activity to the exact task on the project schedule for actuals and project metrics.
- Charts can be produced by process activity, activity group, or piece/parts directly from the time-card system.

I have shown a nine-digit charge number. You may have a different charge numbering system. I hope I've conveyed the concept of what you can do with this. You need to tailor this for your own company's situation. Anyhow, this general format for the change number needs to be institutionalized.

Sometimes, a blow-by-blow description helps cement all this in. I will be revisiting all this later, in Section IV. The description in this chapter will provide some more insight into where I'm heading on this topic.

For my hypothetical company, I am going to assume that I have from 8 to 15 ongoing projects. That tells me that I can assign two digits of my charge number to a project. I will also assume that I can use a circular buffer approach on these two digits; i.e., I will assign numbers from 01 through 99 after which I will cycle back to 01 again. Again, I have purposely stayed away from using 00, which can be used for general (nonproject-specific) stuff.

At this point, I have developed the front end of my charge number heading toward this form:

<Project number><Process activity number>

I can now add in activity identifications. I have set up a complete end-to-end story made up of process activity diagrams (PADs) — one per life-cycle phase in my process repository. I know I have 40* reusable activities whose instances will show up on any project schedule.

The probability of this hypothetical company having more than 99 process activities is extremely small. With this information, I can now determine that two of my numbers within a charge number will be mapped to a process activity. For illustration purposes, I will make this assumption. Your company may choose to allocate three digits for this. Don't get wrapped around the axle about this, however.

In the main process framework model described in Reference 1, I have avoided relating a number to an activity because there are some people out there who view this number as an ordering number — which it isn't. When you use numbers for ordering purposes, you will be saying, for example, that activity 09 is the predecessor to activity 10, etc., which you don't want implied. Also, if you have to add an activity between them (as part of software process improvement), will this new one be numbered 9.5? For this reason, I have been firm about keeping the activity description as an alphabetic description. The number assignment I'm talking about here merely represents an alphabetic description of a portion of a charge number. The operative word here is "number."

At this point, I have established that two of the numbers in any charge number represent the process activity. This mapping is a static mapping from 01 to 99. I have purposely not used 00 because we used that for all the nonscheduled stuff.

A front end of 1510 would tell me this is for project 15 (assigned at enterprise level) and for activity 10 (probably assigned by the software engineering process group [SEPG]) used within that project. Both of these pieces of information are relatively static.

I can now add the piece/part dynamic story.

At this point, we have merely identified the project and the static process activity. A process activity, once placed on a schedule, has two more pieces of information added to it to make it a schedule task; these are as follows:

■ What's the object of the task?
■ Who's responsible for this schedule task?

---

* The number 40 is not unreasonable for a complete engineering life cycle. Some companies may have less, and some may have more.

For any charge number system, we definitely are interested in the former and not in the latter. One company I worked for wanted to add in the "who" part to use it as ammunition against the concerned individual. How's that for killing any initiative! My take on this is, "don't do it." Leave the individual out of this encoding.

For the most part, the object of a task (or instance of a process activity) is a piece/part of your system. This is not a totally true statement, but it's mostly true. For example, if we have a system design and three subsystem designs, there will be four tasks on the schedule (one system and three subsystems) but only one process activity.

This statement is probably going to blow away traditional software project managers: Don't assign dynamic portions of any charge number until you know for sure they exist. You don't know any piece/part of the system exists until after you have executed a "Design Down" kind of activity. What I'm saying here is that on any "Design Down" activity END step, you notify the accounting folks so that they can establish the unfolding charge number. At the end of your system design, you know exactly how many subsystems there are. At the end of any subsystem design, you know exactly how many units there are. The term "unit" could be a C++ class or Ada package, for example. This approach uses the process life-cycle execution itself to drive both follow-on activities and develop the charge number itself via accounting. Your accounting charge number system is totally aligned with your engineering design.

For the piece/part number assignments, these are project dependent. For example, if we started with 1510 and added 3 to get 15103, that has a different meaning than 09103. The former is subsystem 3 related to project 15, and the latter is a different subsystem 3 for project 09.

For companies that are in the system and subsystem design business, I suspect that a single reusable number is quite adequate to represent a system and subsystem. Similar to what was done before, this single number assignment is in the range of 1 through 9. I purposely did not use 0. That use will be dealt with later.

If after doing a "Design Down" on subsystem 3 for project 15, your design comes up with 100 units — then a 3-digit project-dependent number can now be added to the charge number for any given unit. For unit 023, my unfolding charge number is now 15103023, where:

  15 = Project represented by 15 — static part
  10 = Activity 10 — static part
   3 = Subsystem 3 for project 15 — dynamic part
 023 = Unit 023 under subsystem 3 — dynamic part

The astute reader will point out that this is all well and good, but what about the execution of the "Design Down" itself — prior to knowing the number of subsystems (system design) or number of units (subsystem design)? This is where the 0 comes in. Assuming activity 10 was the "Design Down" activity, the folks working a system-level design for project 15 would charge to 15100 ... 0, where:

    15 = Project 15
    10 = Activity 10
     0 = System-level design — implied by 0

Given the same activity and project assumption, the folks working the subsystem 3 design would charge to 15103000, where:

     15 = Project 15
     10 = Activity 10
      3 = Subsystem 3 for project 15
    000 = Subsystem level design — implied by 000

The reader may make another very relevant observation: Because this numbering structure is activity based, we know what activities have what objects. For example, you can't do a "Design Down" activity on a unit object. You can't do an "Implement Unit" activity on a subsystem object. This scheme has a built-in way of validating charge numbers because of this connection to the process world.

If should be clear to you by now that certain activities are more important for SPM than others. The "Design Down" activity is one example. You don't know things such as the following until you execute one of the "Design Down" activities on a schedule:

- The enfolding piece/part story as a result of that design
- Drives further activities on the project schedule
- Drives the enfolding project charge number
- Provides the unfolding integration planning story
- Drives the unfolding piece/part-based SCM repositories

The execution of this particular activity on a schedule gives you a many-for-one sale because of the tight coupling of processes to schedules.

The process model referenced in [1] also considers the integration plan itself to probably be the most important work product you can produce. This is an interesting concept. You actually use the integration plan to drive the schedule. Let's detour a little and look at the integration plan's role in all this:

- After executing a "Design Down" on a subsystem, you know the unit-level piece/part story. These are the actual elements that must be integrated into a total system in some order. This is the time you update your integration plan to address which pieces/parts get integrated first, second, or third, etc., within that subsystem. You update on each subsystem "Design Down" task.
- The resultant integration plan now has an integration roadmap at the unit level. You will see things such as: "Integrate units 3, 4, 7, and 10 first in subsystem ABC, then integrate that base with units 2, 5, 6, 9, and 11, etc." You keep building on the base until everything is integrated.
- Each set of things to be integrated is something I call the "integration set." For the "integrate units" process activity, an object is a pseudo system piece/part — being an integration set coming right out of the integration plan. This plan is used to drive the schedule. From a charge number perspective, we merely need to number the integration sets for charging purposes.

If the integration plan calls for 10 integrations, building progressively upwards on an increasing base, we know we have 10 instances of the single "Integrate Units" process activity on the schedule. The developers need a specific "integration set" object when executing that schedule task. From a charging perspective, we would see something similar to "1524XX …," where:

15 = Project 15
24 = Activity 24 for "Integrate Units"
XX = 01–10 for the 10 integration sets

Integration sets are treated similar to the system object. Similar to the mapping of pieces/parts, accounting needs to extract the integration set identifiers and map it to a charge number. This is a very different role for accounting. This action places accounting as an integral member of the SPM team. Most accounting groups don't do this.

I have advocated a direct alignment of your WBS with your process activities for all the schedulable work. Some readers may take me to task here and remind me that this is a very flat structure — e.g., approximately 40 named process activities for most companies.

You can remedy this flatness very easily. Every process activity has a static belonging to a process group. See Reference [1] for a detailed explanation of process groups. I will give you some examples of process groups that you might want to incorporate into your WBS structure as part of your indentured list of WBS items.

Some examples are as follows:

■ "Design Down" and "Design Unit" may be two of your named process activities that would belong to the "Design" process group.
■ "Integrate Units" and "Test System" may be two of your named process activities that would belong to the "Test" process group.

You could certainly place these process group names for any subtitle in your WBS as follows:

WBS structure
    00 — Nonschedulable items
    …
    01–99 — Schedulable items (activities)
    …
        Design
        18 — Design Down
        23 — Design Unit
        …
        Test
        28 — Integrate Units
        34 — Test System

For my hypothetical company, I have created a structured charge number for schedulable things based on process activities as follows:

<Project ID> ::= 01–99
<Process activity ID>/00 ::= 01–99 (this determines the following structure)
<Variable piece/part or object> ::= 0000–9999
<Rework indicator> ::= 0–9

The maximum numbering representation I've used is a nine-digit charge number. You may use more. You may place your rework indicator elsewhere in this numbering structure.

Tying the charge number and WBS to your schedule tasks and process activities provides incredible SPM metrics for any project. You can determine the following:

- Total effort for a project.
- Work effort by process activity type, i.e., how much was spent on implementation.
- Work effort by process activity group, i.e., how much was spent in all testing activities.
- What was the total effort spent on a particular piece/part of the system?
- What was the pie breakdown on effort on my whole project? How does it relate to industry standards?
- What was my rework costs?
- Show me the chart on all activities organized from most to least. Where did I spend most of my effort? (This gives a big clue to your SEPG people as to which activity to optimize!)

These kinds of metrics results should be maintained and used for subsequent projects. It should provide any software project manager with a wealth of information to get better estimates from past results. With time charge system records in place, you should be able to reconstruct these at a moment's notice.

If you're scratching your head now, don't worry; I'll be explaining this further in Section IV.

Chapter 9

Software Project Management Role Partners Institutionalized

Introduction

In this process-based software process management (SPM) approach, there are definite and directly connected "role players" that cooperate in various ways with the software project manager. These role players are the following:

- Engineering
- Accounting
- Software configuration management (SCM)
- Software quality assurance (SQA)

Unlike traditional methods of SPM, these role players are true partners of SPM — not merely subcontracted helpers hanging around the fringes. This described method has a tight connectivity of process to schedules. This method also has clearly defined expected actions from these role players that are triggered by the END common high-level steps with the "Design Down" schedule tasks. Success depends on each member of the team playing his or her part. The philosophy is very analogous to a surgical team. You certainly need to have a chief surgeon, but you also need operating room nurses and an anesthesiologist for the operation's success. Each has a definite role. Each is expected to perform that role flawlessly and on cue. This same concept applies to effective SPM. This process approach to SPM is not very tolerant of your team players disconnection from you or abdicating their responsibilities to you. Going back to the surgical team analogy, the anesthesiologist does not function according to his or her whim. In surgery, there are certain triggering events that require immediate action. This is true of this process-based SPM approach. We will now look at these triggers for your role partners.

Just go back to Figure 4.8 for a moment. This figure is critical to the understanding of the task–activity relationship. In this chapter, we are concentrating on the right-to-left arrow at the bottom of that figure. The major points to be made are the following:

- Process activities are "what you need to do" process elements.
- Process activities contain high-level steps to be done — some of which are common to all activities.
- Process activities have predecessor/successor relationships to other activities.
- Process activities exist in process activity diagrams (PADs) in the process repository.
- Each PAD represents one phase of the life cycle.
- Activities, once placed on a project schedule, become schedule tasks.
- Project tasks are instances of activities.

Because all tasks on a schedule emanate from one or more activities and because all activities have common high-level steps, it follows that we can connect our role partners via these high-level steps throughout the life cycle.

I described the process activity with its high-level steps at length in Chapter 5. In this chapter, I'm going to concentrate on the END common high-level step as role-partner triggers.

For every activity instance (or schedule task) that is executed, the END high-level step communicates that "doneness" to the various roles. Because the charge number is passed with the END, we can determine the appropriate project, the activity type, the activity object, and whether or not it was a reworked task. In other words, we can tie an END to a particular task in your project schedule. The normal END actions are the following:

- Notify the software project manager that this particular task is done.
- Notify the next activity lead on the schedule that this particular task is done.
- Notify the earned value folks that this particular task is done.
- Possibly notify SQA that this particular task is done (for auditing purposes).
- Possibly notify the development manager that this particular task is done.
- Possibly notify the metrics folks that this particular task is done when passing on the metrics data (if it's a metrics-producing task).

Of all the activities that can be activity instances (or tasks) on a schedule, there are only two activities that are far more important than the others for the software project manager. They are the following:

- The "Design Down" activity
- The "Update Integration Plan" activity

The "Design Down" activity does high-level design that decomposes the target of the design into smaller designed pieces/parts. System design identifies subsystem pieces/parts. Subsystem design identifies unit pieces/parts. Thus, every execution of a "Design Down" done by engineering provides more visibility on the system's hierarchical pieces/parts list. In addition to the standard actions from an END step, this particular activity's END triggers immediate action from the following role partners:

- Engineering — for SPM guidance on unit-based information and early-up developmental units
- Accounting — for charge number elaborations
- SCM — for developmental repository elaborations
- SCM — for sandbox elaborations
- SPM — for schedule planning elaborations

The "Update Integration Plan" activity determines the integration sets (of units) and the integration roadmap ordering. In addition to the standard actions from an END step, this particular activity's END triggers the software project manager to expand the project-planning schedule based on that integration plan. This particular activity is key to intelligent project schedule planning.

Engineering Role Partner Institutionalized

Engineering needs to understand that the high-level designs serve more than one purpose; these purposes include the following:

- Actual flow-down design for the targeted system
- Input to accounting for charge number expansions
- Input to SCM for developmental repository structure expansions (and initial population)
- Input to SCM for project working areas (sandbox) structure creation

Engineering needs to do a thorough job of these decomposing types of designs. All high-level designs in this process-based approach includes the following:

- Identifying the newly designed pieces/parts
- Creating a unique file identifier or a name for each designed element

In addition, those high-level designs that decompose designed elements down to the unit (leaf) level need to add the following pieces of information:

- Whether the unit is to be implemented and unit tested. These tend to be critical units.
- Whether the unit is to be implemented but no unit testing is to be done. These are units where a unit code inspection (built-in) is sufficient or where it makes no sense to develop unit test drivers. Embedded units or units that are not critical quite often fall into this category.
- Whether the unit is reused from before and needs additional code tweaking and a unit test.
- Whether the unit is reused and can be used as is, i.e., without code tweaking and unit testing.
- Finally, which units for any implementation are needed first on the project schedule. Engineering knows this. The software project manager only needs a get-started list of units that, in engineering's judgment, are candidates for early implementation.

All this is valuable information for the software project manager for schedule planning. The last bulleted item provides the software project manager with a get-started lineup of unit-based tasks early-on in the schedule while waiting for the full-blown integration plan that really ties this down for task ordering. This engineering role needs to be institutionalized.

Accounting Role Partner Institutionalized

The END step for any "Design Down" notifies accounting that a high-level design is now done. Accounting now knows the following:

■ The number of designed elements (subsystems or units)
■ The designed elements' names (subsystem names or unit names)

Accounting can now assign codes to each piece/part within the WBS. The WBS structure and format was described in Chapter 8. In addition, accounting is responsible for creating a table relating charge numbers with their breakdown fields. Figure 9.1 shows where the charge number file is located within the project's developmental repository for accounting updates.

The actual charge number file is a multicolumn table relating the charge number (expanded by accounting) to items such as the following:

■ The activity number
■ The activity name
■ The activity object number
■ The activity object name

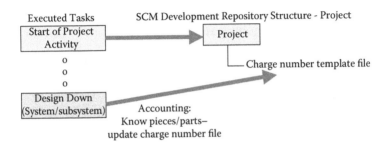

Figure 9.1   SCM development repository buildup for accounting.

Charge #	Activity Number	Activity Name	Activity Object #	Activity Object Name

Figure 9.2   Accounting charge number file for process.

Figure 9.2 shows a representative table to be used for this purpose. I did not show other possible accounting tables to cover the non-activity aspects of any charge number.

Although created by accounting, all the common high-level steps use this file to associate the charge number parameter to their symbolic equivalent fields as part of a graphical user interface (GUI) to the process practitioner. In addition, parameterized filenames will also be accessing this table.

Accounting may not have that role in your company currently. They need to take on this role for this process-based SPM approach. That's why this needs to be institutionalized.

SCM Role Partner Institutionalized

The END step for any "Design Down" activity notifies SCM that a high-level design is now done. SCM also knows the following:

- The number of designed elements (subsystems or units)
- The designed elements names (subsystem names or unit names)

SCM can now take the newly designed names and create another layer of subfolders under the system node or applicable subsystem node for each subsystem and unit, respectively. The developmental repository structure is close to real time and parallels to the high-level design. Once the subfolders have been established, SCM can now populate these subdirectories with appropriate templates and place-holders in readiness for engineering's execution of the next GET high-level step.

As an adjunct to the developmental repository structure getting set up, SCM also needs to expand the project's sandbox. This entails setting up a subfolder for each designed element name under those activities where that type of piece/part is valid. As a reminder, the project's sandbox basic structure was shown in Figure 6.6. For example, if the "Design Down" created units, you would see all the unit names as subfolders under "Implement Unit," "Test Unit," and "Create Unit Test" folders in the sandbox. You would not see unit names under those activities where a unit name was not valid (e.g., "Design Down"). Unlike the developmental repository, the project's sandbox is always a three-layer structure.

SCM is critical for a software project manager in this approach. SCM must move swiftly and act on the END from the "Design Down" task to provide just-in-time support for the software project manager and engineering to keep going on the project schedule. It is for these reasons that SCM's actions must be institutionalized.

SPM Role Partner Institutionalized

The END step for any "Design Down" notifies the software project manager that a high-level design is now done. Just as the other role partners, the software project manager knows the following:

- The number of designed elements (subsystems or units)
- The designed elements' names (subsystem names or unit names)

This provides the check-off list for the software project manager to account for on the project schedule.

If the "Design Down" happens to be a subsystem design down to the unit level, the software project manager is provided a lot more information:

- Whether the unit is to be implemented and unit tested
- Whether the unit is to be implemented but no unit testing is to be done
- Whether the unit is reused and needs additional code tweaking and a unit test
- Whether the unit is reused and can be used as is
- Finally, which are the units for early implementation on the project schedule

The software project manager can take the information from the last bulleted item, qualified by the earlier bulleted items, and place it all on the planning schedule immediately. This information comes directly from engineering's high-level design activity.

Later, when the integration plan has been completed (triggered by the END on "Update Integration Plan"), the software project manager can completely order the entire planning schedule based on the parts list from design and ordering direction from the integration plan. The resultant planning schedule is totally aligned with the engineering design and integration plans. The SPM actions here need to be institutionalized.

SQA Role Partner Institutionalized

The END step for any "Design Down" notifies SQA that a high-level design is now done. SQA has a role to check the integrity of the SCM repository and sandbox area as a quality function. SQA could also perform a quality check on the accounting charge number file if it is so desired. It is critical that both be set up accurately.

PRE-EXECUTION SEGMENT

Chapter 10

Preproposal

Introduction

This book does not have a primary focus on all that needs to be done prior to issuing a proposal for bid work. Having said that, it does after considerable guidance on what that entails on the Web. I ran across a very comprehensive business development (BD) process chart [2] that provides almost 100 steps or mind-jogger items that need to be considered for a BD process. This particular chart is a marvelous aid if you really want process guidance in that area.

When does software project management (SPM) show up in the life cycle? I mention this because, believe it or not, I have been at companies that could not give you a straight answer on this. Many places I worked would look you right in the eye and tell you a project starts when they get paid for a go-ahead. All the work that happened before was not a real project. Huh! The effort was real. The manpower was real. The costs were real.

If you look at the entire pre-execution segment, all the phases up to the proposal phase are inherently both of the following:

- They are BD oriented.
- They have an enterprise or business focus that just happens to be related to the proposed project.

Most companies tend to separate out charges during this period because the BD focus really applies potentially to a lot of projects within some sphere. From a process perspective, we still:

- Execute process activities (tasks)
- Execute event-driven procedures
- Need some kind of version-controlled repository
- Need some kind of activity-based "sandbox"
- Need charge numbers

The only difference is that these efforts are not project related — they are enterprise BD related. In this process-based SPM approach, we really need the same kinds of things during BD as we do elsewhere. We need the same:

- Life-cycle mapping described in Chapter 4
- Process activity connectivity to "how-to's" described in Chapter 5
- Institutionalized considerations described in Chapter 7 through Chapter 9

We don't need Chapter 6, because the special process activities only show up during the execution segment.

The big difference in this BD world is that although there are costs incurred, they are not specific to any given project to a large extent. The costs here are better extrapolated to the real projects. Remember, you may execute the BD part of your life cycle many times more than you have real projects for execution. Any one pass through BD may not have a resultant project to associate charges against.

No matter how many false starts you may have during BD, the costs should be accounted for as part of your overhead expenses. I have been at companies that would go after anything that passes the door. These are either very hungry companies or very stupid ones. You can literally "go under" if you spend precious resources and time on things that have a minimal-to-no-chance of winning. It is beyond the scope of this book, but if you're in that situation, you really need to look at your long-term and short-term strategic plans as to what business you're really in. I've had to deal with this very subject as an independent consultant. I consider myself a "process guy" who places an emphasis on software process architecture and deployment. I happen to believe that a solid process foundation directly supports major roles such as SPM, engineering, software configuration management

(SCM), and software quality assurance (SQA). That same solid process foundation makes CMMI compliance and ISO 9001 certification a slam dunk. I don't go after consulting jobs that do not match my capabilities. It's true for an individual. It's true for a company.

Throughout this book, I have described how connecting processes to the wonderful world of SPM has incredible value. Everything prior to the proposal phase has, as its goal, the production of a proposal for a "win." That final proposal has a plan that gets submitted to your customer. In the SPM planning world, I want to make it really clear that there are two SPM plans you need to develop; these are the following:

▪ One plan exists to support your bid position. This plan is an educated guess based on experience and past history and is primarily done for the customer. It is that plan that hopefully gets more and more refined on other projects as we get better estimations based on prior actuals. I call this first plan the "external" plan. This plan is for the customer. All the pre-proposal efforts are meant to culminate in that bid submission.
▪ Another plan is developed that is used for tracking progress purposes. I will show you that you can't do all of this plan up front. At best, you can get an understanding of requirements and make clarification where necessary, plus have a very top-level design approach developed at proposal time. Of all the parts of this plan, the engineering part is the most unknown. You can only determine the very early part up to the high-level design and then you have to fill out the remainder after you actually do that design, etc., at execution time. I call this second plan the "internal" plan. This plan is for tracking purposes. At pre-proposal time, the best you have that may "stick" for planning or tracking purposes are the following:
  – All the contract stuff related to reviews, meetings, etc.
  – Known deliverables.
  – Internal company-imposed project management requirements.
  – Engineering actions up to high-level design.
  Beyond that you know nothing.

Many software project managers are confused about this basic premise. Many software project managers I have known consider the first plan (i.e., the one for the customer) to be the same plan you track against. How crazy is that! You are almost guaranteed to be tracking reality (execution results) against fiction (the guesswork done earlier). This is the one area in which I've personally seen software project managers come unglued when reality doesn't match up with the earlier guess-based plan. As mentioned before, an extreme case of this occurred when the software project manager became so irate that the developers had to placate this person and force the execution-time piece/part story to be the same as the guessed piece/part story. This action ended up with disastrous results.

When there is interest in bidding for a project, an SPM presence shows up — even if it's in a subservient role. The bid process is pretty standard for government-contracting companies, whereas the equivalent shows up in commercial companies when features or capabilities are being seriously considered for near-term release.

Think about the following:

- You are following a process to do the pre-proposal world. This is where the BD reference chart [2] would help.
- You are following some kind of pre-execution schedule for doing work. You may not have a formal schedule in the execution sense, but you still need some kind of roadmap during this time.
- You are heading toward that go/no-go decision point (gate activity) to proceed (or not proceed) with an actual proposal.
- You're spending company money that needs to be recouped over time so that you stay in business.

Sometimes the "proposal manager" is not only the person responsible for getting the proposal out but he or she may also be the candidate who executes the SPM. I maintain that a process is a process. We have pre-execution segment processes and execution segment processes. Although the skill set of the former is more marketing oriented than the latter, there is a lot of overlap for both segments — especially with engineering.

There is something to be said for having a pre-execution segment "project manager" whose team includes the proposed software project manager. Engineering designs (and development) are the major differences that show up between pre-execution and execution segments. You do not want to promise engineering directions at pre-execution time that an execution-time engineering component could not embrace or "run with." If you don't do this, there may be a tendency for the proposal-time software project manager to promise all kinds of things,

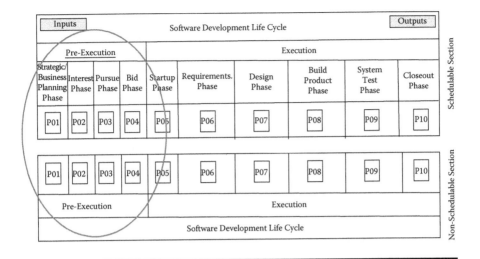

Figure 10.1   Pre-execution life-cycle guidance.

knowing full well that he or she is not going to have to manage the "real thing" later. This will turn out to be a classic "good luck to you" approach to SPM.

Using the Process for Pre-execution Direction

I have subdivided the pre-execution segment into the following phases:

- Strategic or business planning phase
- Interest (opportunity) phase
- Pursue phase
- Bid phase

The first three items reflect pre-proposal efforts (i.e., they have a business focus). The last item is where we actually produce a proposal (i.e., it has a project focus). This is shown in Figure 10.1.

It is in these first three phases (prior to proposal) that you will see the gate activity within a phased process activity diagram (PAD). I had introduced you to this kind of activity in Figure 5.1 (triangle icon), showing it in a phase PAD, and also in Figure 5.4, showing what a gate activity detail would resemble on the Web. These gate activities are at the end of a phase, indicating some kind of go/no-go action. I hope that you will readily see that after going through an interest (opportunity) phase, you may or may not proceed with any proposal.

In Figure 10.1, I have highlighted that part of the developmental life cycle in which you take your process guidance. There are some other things to be noted in that figure as follows:

- The entire life cycle is made up of two segments:
  - Pre-execution
  - Execution
- The pre-execution segment is made up of four phases that I've already described.
- The execution segment is made up of six phases:
  - Start-up phase
  - Requirements phase
  - Design phase
  - Build product phase
  - System test phase
  - Closeout phase
- All phases, segments, and the entire life cycle also have a bottom section to accommodate event-driven procedures related to their respective scopes.
- The top-left and top-right corners show all the inputs and outputs for the entire life cycle.

You may have a different set of phases and segments in your life cycle. If you were to click on the pre-execution segment hyperlink, it would take you to Figure 10.2.

This drilldown just presents the phases pertinent to the pre-execution segment. At this point, we still don't see any "meat." As an example, if you were to drill down on the interest phase hyperlink, you would see a Web page that looks similar to Figure 10.3.

It is at the phase level that you'll see the activity-flow meat. Please notice that the inputs and outputs are strictly for that phase. Also notice that there are five regular activities and a gate activity. Two of the activities can be done concurrently, if manpower resources allow.

The point of all of this is that you take all your direction from the pre-execution segment of the life cycle. It will show you the following:

- All the "what you have to do" tasks
- The how-to procedures that elaborate on the high-level steps inside each activity
- The inputs and outputs by activity, phase, and segment
- Any event-driven procedural how-to actions that may be needed

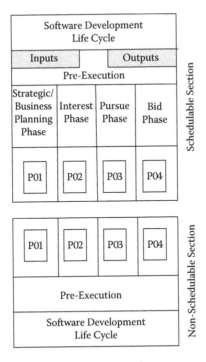

Figure 10.2   Pre-execution segment.

This is no different from the direction you would take while executing a project.

In other words, it is all laid out for you to follow. Each pre-execution activity that you're working should use the AVG (average) estimate when this part of your nonpaid work is being performed. Remember, AVG is not the loaded-average version (L-AVG) used when in the execution portion of your life cycle. When you complete the work represented by all the activities in this pre-execution segment, you can update your estimates (and in particular the AVG) with actuals for better work estimates on future endeavors.

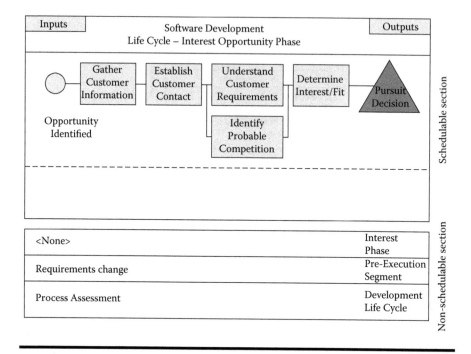

Figure 10.3   Interest opportunity phase.

Chapter 11

Proposal

Introduction

The proposal phase is really the first phase that is project specific but not paid. Payment is made only after project award. All phases prior to the proposal phase are essentially enterprise-based with a slight project perspective. It is in this phase that we could set up some basic project-related repositories to ensure that proposal artifacts get carried forward into the execution segment.

At proposal time, there are some major factors that will drive the software project management (SPM) plan in relation to the external customer:

- An understanding of the target customer requirements after normalization and clarification
- An understanding of the contract customer requirements after normalization and clarification
- Deliverables
- Execution of a top-level design approach, as provided in the proposal response

From these factors, the primary schedule-related end results you want to achieve at this early stage are as follows:

- Duration in calendar units (weeks/months/etc.)
- Rough planning package distribution across that time span
- Manpower estimates across that span

This rough picture certainly converts to a dollar equivalent for internal costing and external pricing. This rough roadmap may be based on the customer's own directives or your own competencies in regard to the staffing situation. At this point, the customer may ask for capabilities to be delivered over time. That directive converts to an incremental developmental life cycle. If the customer wants a full-blown system all at once, it will convert to a waterfall model for your developmental life cycle. Typically, at this stage, you don't calendarize your rough durational schedule unless the customer has so specified.

Let's now turn our attention to the process drivers that produce this external plan. This part of any life cycle has diametrically opposing goals:

■ You need to have enough information to create this external plan, yet you don't want to spend too much time and effort as freebie time, i.e., time not paid for.
■ You want information derived at this stage to be used as a head start if you actually get this project to execute, but you want to restrict that information to really useful execution-time information.

In my experience, I have seen companies come to these rough schedules from the following:

■ Wild guesses
■ Rounded-off numbers
■ Past experience
■ Lines of code estimates
■ Function point analysis
■ To fit customer's expectations

In this process-based approach to SPM, this early part of the life cycle is spelled out in your early process activity diagram (PAD). You should have a process activity called "Set Up Project" that contains, among other things, these two high-level steps:

■ Set up charge numbers.
■ Set up software configuration management (SCM) repository.

I remind the reader that activities are schedulable tasks — what you need to do — and high-level steps are actions that we absolutely, positively want people to do. With these steps in a process activity that, in turn, are shown in your early PAD, you are guaranteeing repeatability in accomplishing early SPM efforts. With these steps in place, you can use them as "hooks" to any how-to procedural element if you want to spell that out.

By the time you get to a proposal phase, you are really interested in being a candidate for execution selection. Companies tend not to expend dollars on any proposal unless there is a good probability of a win situation. Software proposals can be extremely expensive if you're just doing it for a drill.

I have certainly been involved in huge proposal efforts in the U.S. Department of Defense (DoD) contracting world. In that environment, you really need to pay attention to customer requirements for the following:

- Proposal requirements (for the proposal itself)
- Target-system requirements for the proposed end product

Both tend to be collated, gathered, and distributed to the proposal writers. If I were assigned certain sections, I would be provided with storyboard themes and requirements that must be accounted for in my presented proposal product and proposal end-product descriptions. I've seen problems with requirements at this stage because not enough effort was spent normalizing and clarifying requirements. I will talk about requirements a lot, as well as why it is important to thoroughly understand requirements during this phase.

This process-based approach deals with the proposal requirements (for the proposal itself) via the following:

- High-level activity steps within the proposal phase
- Elaborated procedural support for high-level steps with any activity
- Possible event-driven procedures whose scope is the proposal phase

In other words, all the necessary tasks and actions come from the process life cycle Web representation. All activities in the pre-execution segment should clearly be identified as pre-execution types of activities. Later, we want to add up all the work expended on our own dime and include it in our overhead-loading factor (refer back to Chapter 7 for the L-AVG determination). It is especially true during the proposal

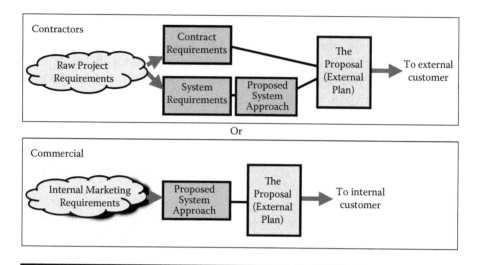

Figure 11.1   The SPM big picture for proposals.

phase because we do gross-level tasks similar to what goes in during the execution segment. In Figure 10.3, if I had expanded the "proposal phase" versus the "interest opportunity" phase, you would see the lineup of schedulable activities supporting proposal development. The execution results of those activities provide the proposed target-system information to the customer.

The focus of this book is more on the target-system aspects of the proposal and the relationship of the proposal efforts to the execution segment of the life cycle. Processes fit into this phase in these areas:

- SCM proposal-time repository that feeds into execution-time developmental repository
- Life-cycle activities for completeness and repeatability
- Deliverable alternative customer pricing for real versus virtual documents
- Process-based estimations as an adjunct to other estimation techniques
- Get-started execution planning schedule
- Controlling requirements
- Process flow down to proposed subcontractors

In Figure 11.1, I have shown the 40,000-ft view of the proposal phase from two different points of view.

Figure 11.1 is really a top-half extraction of Figure 1.1 and Figure 1.2. It is important to focus in on the proposal part of the pre-execution segment from a government contractor perspective and a commercial perspective. I realize I have taken tremendous liberties with these views because commercial requirements almost always call for elaborations first, even before you can start. As I mentioned earlier, a commercial requirement in the cellular base station world, "we need roaming" is hardly anything to go on in its present form. Conversely, government requirements tend to be quite disciplined stipulations ("shall ...").

The biggest difference (from that 40,000-ft perspective) in these two worlds, deals with the presence or absence of contract requirements. Commercial requirements almost never include these at all. The biggest detail that marketers want to know from engineering is regarding the question, "when can you do it?" Government stipulations include both contract requirements and target-system needs.

The biggest dilemma in SPM at proposal time is that you need to do enough to accurately estimate the scope of work in all its facets and yet don't do too much on your own dime. It's a huge balancing act at this time in the life cycle.

For government contractors, here is the good news about contract requirements:

■ They are usually self explanatory.
■ They can be accounted for and placed on your proposal schedule and applied totally in your execution schedule — if you get chosen for that execution.

I must admit I tend to look at all requirements as candidates for normalization and clarification. Although not explicitly shown, it is my contention that you really need to massage requirements from their "raw" state for both environments. If these terms seem strange to you, don't be alarmed; I will be discussing requirements a lot, later in this chapter. This is the one area that can really sabotage your efforts if you don't pay attention to requirements.

Some other things to note about Figure 11.1 for both environments are the following:

■ Both will go through efforts to come up with a target-system approach. The formality of this may vary, but it still happens.
■ Both produce some kind of proposal to the customer. In the government arena, the customer is external, and the proposal is formal. For commercial companies, the customer tends to be internal marketing, and the proposal is very informal.

Be aware that at this early stage of the SPM plan, you may or may not do any rough-level design at all. You may extract information from a past project. You simply cannot assume that some level of design is going to happen — on your own dime. You can assume that, no matter what, you need a clear understanding of the job at hand via the requirements definition.

I have some ambivalence on this topic. You could certainly make the argument that you really do need a rough design from the system to subsystem level at this point in time. If you do a rough design, it means that you are executing a form of "Design Down" activity at proposal time (term suggested: "P-Design Down," the pre-execution form). Be aware that this effort is an overhead function. You are not compensated for this at all. For those who do this, you need to capture your top-level designs in your SCM developmental repository. If you take this route, the term *design* would also mean, possibly, allocating requirements down to those newly designed pieces/parts. Do you really want to do this on your own money? At this stage, I would suggest just a rough-level design and no allocations of requirements. Leave that for paid work.

Unlike homebuilders, software builders may or may not know where certain functionalities or capabilities reside? Homebuilders know that the cooking capability goes in the kitchen and the bathing or showering capability goes in a bathroom. For certain industries with an extensive wealth of experience behind them, they may know which capability goes where in the system. When I worked in the cellular telecommunications industry, it was well known what goes in a cell phone versus a cell tower versus a base station controller. For new software development, that might be pushing the envelope, because you may not know where all this resides.

My pitch to software project managers at this point in time is this: if you are not absolutely certain of your capability mappings in regard to your system components, don't go ahead! Do not attempt that mapping or keep those capability mappings to a really high level. I have personally witnessed an ugly scene when the proposal-time system picture turned out to be different from the real picture after execution. Your customer will be left wondering if you really know what you're doing. Again, don't do this.

There's a lot of work done during proposal time. It's absolutely foolish not to capture that work as a foundation for execution — if execution is to occur. I have worked at several companies that treated proposal stuff as just something to get business in the door. Once awarded, it becomes an attitude of the kind, "let's do it for real now."

I can also tell you from personal experience that I would have loved to know what design trade-offs and decisions occurred at proposal time to come up with the presented design. This information doesn't show up in the customer proposal. This information is behind-the-scenes kind of stuff that would sure be useful to the execution team.

A pet peeve of mine relates to costs and pricing. There may have been a conscious effort to low-bid the project to get a foot in the door for some marketplace. This low bid may have little to no relevance to the estimated cost, duration, and manpower estimates. I have known software project managers who flog the development staff to meet the proposed price goals even though it's totally fictitious compared to estimated costs. If you have an 18-month-estimated period of performance but tell the customer it will be done in 12 months, it is not fair to beat up engineering when schedules exceed the one-year mark. It is this kind of behavior that does not endear a software project manager to engineering. Guess what happens on the next project for this manager — no one believes the individual and they will make no effort to meet SPM deadlines. I have seen this more times than I care to think about. The point here is that estimated costs are valid to be communicated to the execution team — not the price.

Proposal Repository

As you are developing any proposal, there is a need to capture all details, so that you can get a leg up on all this at execution time. Figure 11.2 shows a top-level view of such a proposal repository.

If you haven't realized this before, this is a SCM issue. You certainly need a root node for the project itself. Under that root node, you need

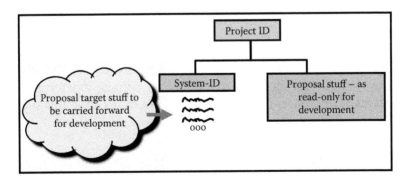

Figure 11.2   Proposal SCM repository top-level structure.

a subfolder for the target system and one for proposal work products. There are some points to be made about Figure 11.2:

- Ideally this repository is a version-controlled repository using a "check-in" or "checkout" kind of accessibility.
- Ideally this repository becomes the developmental repository once you win the execution.

The following proposal work products need to be carried forward into the execution segment if you get a job award:

- Design trade-offs
- Design decisions/rationale
- Processed requirements from proposal phase
- Estimated duration of performance costs
- Estimated manpower costs.

If at all possible, your actual proposal-time design should be placed under the system subfolder as a version 0 file. The design trade-offs and decisions stay under the proposal subfolder, because they are behind-the-scenes kinds of work products. The processed requirements should have been divided into contract and target-system requirements at proposal time. Contract requirements go under the "Project ID" subfolder, and target-system requirements go under the "System ID" subfolder. If you are processing requirements via a tool such as DOORS, an attribute field can handle this division.

The bottom line is that you want the repository at proposal time to be your base repository at execution time. You want to end up with a base structure as shown in Figure 11.3.

This structure is all set to add subsystem subfolders later when we do the real design at execution time. The reader might question why we don't set up subsystem subfolders right now at proposal time. After all, didn't we do a rough design identifying those subsystems? The answer is that we may have different lineups at execution time and at proposal time. It may be a mistake to do this lower-level structure too early. Let the "Design Down" executions definitely determine your subsystems at execution time; i.e., use the process to drive this structure.

Requirements

As mentioned before, you need to do enough to understand the scope of the work, but you also need to recognize what can be done at

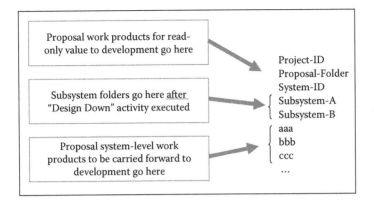

Figure 11.3   Top-level repository structure at proposal time.

execution time, when you're getting paid for your efforts. This is far from a perfect approach, but, in general, I have found that you really need to break down all your customer requirements into discrete units at proposal time — both contract and target-system requirements. If you don't, you may miss some vital requirements that elude your cost estimates for inclusion. There are companies out there that choose to do selective normalization, superimposing a judgment call on what requirements affect cost. That's a balancing act decision that may still hurt you if you miss something.

For those of you in the commercial world, you may have to elaborate your customer requirements to even get to a starting position. The example that I mentioned before (we need roaming) is hardly a basis for requirements when you get this kind of input from marketing. This is where your technical people come in to create a set of high-level requirements that reflect the marketing need. Hopefully, these same technical folks will create normalized/clarified requirements because that's an in-house operation that is under your control. Figure 11.4 shows this flow for commercial environments.

I really recommend that you retain the "raw" customer requirements as is within your requirement tool. You always want to go back to the customer-supplied requirement in the form it was in. This serves as your top-layer for traceability and volatility of requirements when changes occur.

Normalization is the act of decomposing raw customer requirements into discrete units. English can be a terrible language to describe requirements as the language is not exact. In mathematics, we can write formulas with precedence semantics built into the formula. No

Figure 11.4   Requirements normalization flow.

such exactness occurs in the English language. We are at the mercy of whoever wrote the customer requirement for its true meaning.

At normalization time, we can certainly subdivide (and mark) the requirements into two categories:

■ Contract requirements
■ Target-system requirements

I have found that full normalization of contract requirements seems to be appropriate at proposal time. You could certainly make the case that some normalization could be held off until execution time if you truly believe that it's not a cost driver at proposal time. I favor complete normalization at proposal time just to make good and sure that nothing falls through the cracks that might affect our costing efforts. Normalization effort can be very distributed and done by a lot of people. You really want English majors, for instance, but not technical people (except as needed), for this drill. If you do this right, normalization can be done very quickly.

I thought it worthwhile to show the readers some examples of normalized requirements.

Figure 11.5 shows one such example in which the incoming requirement was really four separate and distinct requirements. This is a real-world example at one company in which I worked. This company did not do requirements normalization and missed the part about demonstrating the product. That was an expensive oversight. In this example, all four normalized requirements would trace back to the original customer-supplied requirement.

Figure 11.6 shows an "or" list example.

The wording on the customer-supplied requirement has a list of items that has an "or" to be incorporated. In this example, this single requirement is good as is. It doesn't need normalization. As crazy as this sounds, I have marked this as "normalized" even though it's exactly

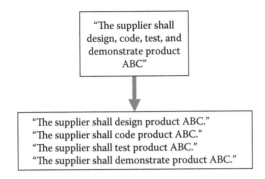

Figure 11.5   Requirements normalization example 1.

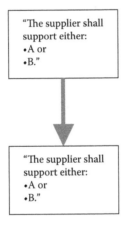

Figure 11.6   Requirements normalization example 2.

the same as the customer-supplied requirement. By providing that traceability, I have also identified this one as being processed.

If you look at Figure 11.7, you have an example of an all-inclusive list that can be normalized.

Because both list items need doing, we can convert this single requirement into two normalized requirements as shown.

Figure 11.8 shows why English is a horrible language for describing requirements.

Is it (A and B) or (C and D)? Is it A and (B or C) and D? Is it ((A and B) or C) and D? Is it something else? This customer-supplied requirement is totally ambiguous as written. You need to go back to the customer for intent on this one.

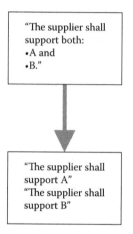

Figure 11.7   Requirements normalization example 3.

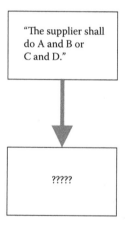

Figure 11.8   Ambiguous normalization example 4.

Once you've normalized the requirements, you now need to clarify ambiguous requirements or open-ended requirements to make them unambiguous. It is in this area that the commercial company has a distinct advantage over the government contractor world. When you run across ambiguous requirements in the commercial world, you can quite often merely ask your customer what that meant. Government contractors don't have that luxury and need to create default clarifications to proceed with proposal costing. Default clarifications can be changed for intent and cost once the actual customer delineates those

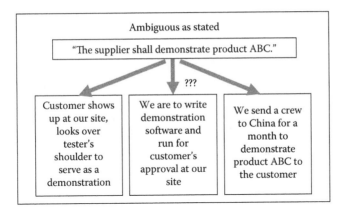

Figure 11.9   Requirements clarification example 1.

intents. You can always smile and say, "We made a cost estimate based on clarification X. If you want clarification Y, there are some cost/time adjustments that may need to be made."

There is a huge caveat with clarification that needs to be made regarding proposal-time efforts. It is quite satisfactory to impose judgment calls on what needs to be clarified now versus later. You certainly want to clarify ambiguous requirements at proposal time if there is a cost impact involved. It is quite acceptable not to clarify ambiguous requirements when a judgment is made in which there are no cost impacts. These types of requirements mostly show up as target-system requirements. When you think about it, design itself is a clarifying type of activity. It is unrealistic to think that we can clarify all things at proposal time. In a fencing job, for example, if your customer wanted three 2x4 boards between posts, it is ambiguous about their position placement but not for a board count. You could defer clarifying whether the 2x4s are flat or on end to a later stage. There is no cost impact involved at proposal time.

Figure 11.9 shows a clarification example that was a real-world requirement.

A normalized requirement such as the one in Figure 11.9 cries out for clarification. I just showed three clarification possibilities. The cost and effort differences are enormous if you leave this kind of requirement unclarified. At one place I worked, I was actually in a meeting with company management and customer management that almost turned into a fistfight over requirement–intent differences. The company could have acted in one of two ways to mitigate this kind of trauma:

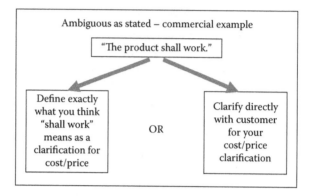

Figure 11.10   Requirements clarification example 2.

- If you can't close the loop with the customer at proposal time, at least pick a clarification position and cost it. At least you have a shot at revisiting this clarification for some other intent with its associated cost/effort adjustments.
- Close the loop with the customer at proposal time and agree on the correct clarification for cost/effort.

By the way, a customer meeting early on to go over any and all clarifications is very worthwhile if it is allowed. Your customer will love you for it. You get to do it correctly, out of the box. This is a veritable win-win situation. I actually suggested an off-site meeting for this at one commercial company. I received puzzled looks in response that seemingly said, "who is this person?" You want to increase the "yes" requirement items and decrease the "but" requirement items. Test time is not the time to be arguing about requirements and their intent.

I have added another clarification example in Figure 11.10 for you to see.

This was an actual acceptance type of customer requirement given to us related to a program of the small file transfer kind. This is another example of a requirement that cries out for clarification. I actually asked the software lead what he thought "will work" means? He told me that if we could transfer X number of 80 character records and Y number of binary 512 records successfully, he would consider that as meeting the "will work" definition. We clarified that acceptance as per the lead's call on this and fed it back to the customer. We ended up getting customer approval of that clarification quite early. There was absolutely no ambiguity about acceptance criteria because we did this.

Other Considerations

There are several other topics that need to be covered as they relate to this process-based approach to software project management:

- Documents preparation
- Process as an estimation tool
- Subcontract management

Even today, there are many software companies that are essentially in the documentation business rather than in the software business. I make a big distinction between these two terms:

- Documentation
- Documents

You want to do the former, and you want less of the latter. Software engineers are notorious for not being good at English grammar and spelling. Why do we have these types of people writing documents? They are not good at it and don't like it. I don't know about you, but this is a recipe for failure in my book. Software engineers view document preparation as the dreary part of their job. You make your software engineers really happy when you reduce the drudgery of their job so that they can concentrate on computer science stuff. They love that world of programming. At a large telecommunications company, their software workforce was mostly made up of engineers for whom English was their second language. How crazy it is to have these people write documents!

My process architectural model (the basis of this book) has a strong bias toward building work products from each and every activity — not documents. This was done on purpose.

Figure 11.11 shows the scenario in which you have many work products contained in a document.

Documents have a table of contents that essentially states that Chapter 1 contains this kind of stuff, Chapter 2 has that kind of stuff, and so on. Many documents need to copy from one or more work products and paste that information into the pretty print. It's my claim that you have now violated the basic database rule relating to a single information source. For documents, you have one source as a work product and a copy in time of that same source in the document. Notice I said "in time." If that work product was information in a tool, you will end up with the tool getting updated whereas the document

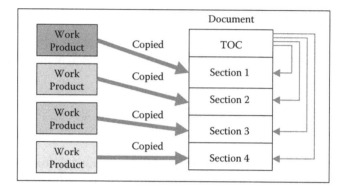

Figure 11.11   Typical document production.

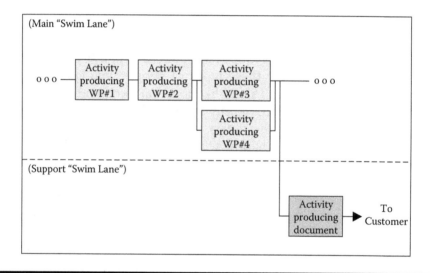

Figure 11.12   Document preparation from a process perspective.

is not updated. You may have a situation in which some engineers are looking at the document whereas others are looking at the tool. How's that for introducing defects into your developmental life cycle!

In each and every PAD, I have shown a dotted line dividing the main line activities from the support activities. I called these *swim lanes*. Let's now turn our attention to Figure 11.12 for an elaboration of why we need a swim lane.

If you had to really produce a document in pretty print, that activity would show up in the support swim lane. In Figure 11.12, I show four main line activities producing work products 1 through 4. I show

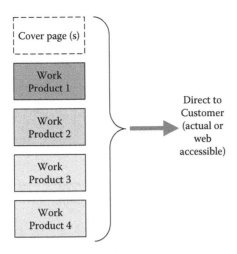

Figure 11.13   Virtual document submission.

the document-producing activity after all four work products are done. People such as technical editors, who worry about headers, footers, margins, styles, bulleted lists, etc., do this activity. They are much better at doing it than your software engineers. Also, this document-producing activity can be separated for your customer at an alternate cost and price. You smile and tell your customer, "We can produce virtual documents for you at no charge or a real document for $x." You'd be surprised how many customers will opt for the cheaper solution.

What is a virtual document? Let's look at Figure 11.13.

This example showed this virtual document as being made up of a cover page (or pages) followed by four work products. You might imagine that WP1 is a Microsoft Word file, WP2 is a Microsoft Excel file, WP3 is a Microsoft PowerPoint file, and WP4 is a Microsoft Project file. At one company, we actually sent five separate files to the customer as a virtual document. If you use standard Microsoft Office products, the customer prefers to open up WP2 with his Microsoft Excel application rather than looking at a PDF type of file. Because work products are natural outputs from activities, there is no cost to this type of document. You don't take the time to copy, and you retain the single source for information at the same time. Think about virtual documents as a freebie option for your customer versus an added cost/price for a real document. As an aside, I cringe when software engineers take their inputs from a document. I keep telling them that it is at best a snapshot in time and may not be correct.

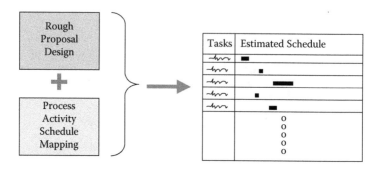

Figure 11.14   Use process as an estimation tool.

I want to switch topics now and look at the process itself as an estimation tool. I am not suggesting this as your one-and-only estimation method. It has definite value in validating (or not validating) any estimation technique you have used.

If you step back and look at the very essence of estimating work, you would notice that it involves breaking activities down to manageable chunks for estimation and rolling those estimates up to form that big picture. Work can be sequential. Work can have predecessor/successor relationships to other work. Work can be concurrent. Work can have dependencies on other work, etc. Haven't I just described the schedulable activities in each PAD over a life cycle? It is on this basis that I am promoting the process model itself as a marvelous estimating tool. The process model has the following elements:

■ Activities what you need to do linked with other activities representing predecessor/successor relationships
■ PADs containing activities
■ Life cycle containing a set of PADs

In Chapter 7, I introduced you to the concept of the L-AVG for each activity type. The term L-AVG is the average effort to do this type of activity with a loading factor added to it. From a SPM perspective, I can lay out my projected work based on the process roadmap and on the rough proposal design, and get loaded times for each and every activity for rolling up estimates. I show this graphically in Figure 11.14.

What may not be intuitively obvious about this figure is that the front end of this estimation drill can be totally lifted as a "get-started" execution schedule. There are some things we can lift for certain and some that we can't. Because we haven't done a real-world systems-

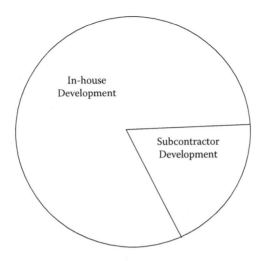

Figure 11.15 Proposed work — inside/outside efforts.

level design (that's an execution activity), we can't carry forward anything past the "Design Down (system)" activity. But we can carry forward everything up to that point to get a head start on the real execution-time schedule. This is a veritable two-for-one sale.

I'd like to talk about subcontracted work now and its relationship to the process model described.

It has always amazed me how subcontractors and in-house workers are treated differently. If you think about work, people wearing a blue badge or a red badge do it. It really doesn't matter who does the work. What does matter is each of the following:

- Allocated requirements for the work
- Schedules for the work
- Acceptance criteria to consider the work "done"

An internal worker should have the same exit criteria imposed as an external worker. If you think of all work as a pie, then a slice of that pie may be allocated to a subcontractor. This is shown in Figure 11.15.

No matter what, you want exit criteria, acceptance, quality, and configuration controls.

For many government contractors, the government demands that you flow down processes to your subcontractors. This process model really stands out in this area. Let's see Figure 11.16.

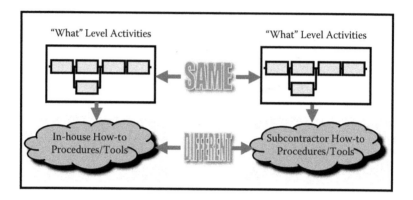

Figure 11.16 Process activities flowed down to subcontractors.

Because we have a definite "what" and "how" separation in the process model, we can actually flow down all the PADs (with their activities) to a subcontractor as is. It should be totally portable at this level. No matter which badge you're wearing, you do design, coding, testing, etc. What is different is at the how-to level. Your subcontractors have their own procedures and toolsets that are probably different from what you have. That's OK. From a software quality assurance (SQA) subcontractor selection perspective, you merely want to confirm that they have an equivalent how-to connection to the high-level steps for schedulable work and an equivalent set of event-driven procedures that you show. SQA can now use the process model as the basis for subcontractor selection. The process model facilitates subcontractor process flow down for the government very well. For large term contracts, you can even incorporate subcontractor process offerings right into your own intranet process displays. Pretty exciting, eh?

I hope you realize that this same figure cannot only be used for subcontractor process flow down, but the same process portability can also be applied to the following:

- Different sites within your own company, both domestic and international
- Acquired companies

In Chapter 3 and Chapter 5, I introduced you to the model itself. This "what"-level portability can easily use "how" selectors that would direct you to things such as the San Diego how-to option versus the Texas how-to option.

Similar to the pre-proposal part of the pre-execution segment, you can update all the AVG estimates for each activity used and update them with new actuals. This way, you get better and better estimates for these pre-execution work activities on the next go-around.

I realize that there is a whole lot more to say about proposals. I highlighted the aspects of proposal efforts as it relates to this process architectural model approach to SPM.

EXECUTION
SEGMENT

Chapter 12

Project Setup

Introduction

There are some things that you need to set up for this process-based software project management (SPM) approach. These fall into two categories:

- Enterprise setup level
- Project setup level

Section III talked about all systems that needed to be institutionalized (or set up) at the enterprise level. In this chapter, I will address project-specific items that need to be set up.

At this point in the life cycle, you are now being paid. At this stage you should have the following enterprise structures:

- Process repository institutionalized
- Script programming institutionalized for process practitioners
- Inspection procedure institutionalized along with inspection checklists for quality
- Activity estimations established
- Work breakdown structure (WBS) and charge number foundation structures in place
- Software project management (SPM) role partners set up and trained

In addition, having gone through the proposal phase, you should have the following project foundation items set up and established:

- Proposal repository structure populated with proposal work products
- Requirements normalized and partially clarified

We now have to do these at the project level:

- Establish the process basis for this project's execution.
- Convert the proposal repository to the developmental repository.
- Populate the developmental repository with known templates and placeholders at the project and system levels. This includes all deliverables.
- Establish the project's sandbox.
- Establish the project release repository.
- Establish the static portion of the project's charge numbers.
- Establish the beginning planning schedule from the proposal schedule basis.
- Add real calendar dates to that schedule.
- Add any outstanding contract events to the schedule.
- Identify project members.

Clearly there are more line items to set up (i.e., office space, labs, etc.). I chose not to deal with these matters as they are beyond the scope of this book.

Process Basis

I hope to refresh your memory regarding this topic. If your process elements have been done correctly, they should all be as follows:

- Version controlled in the process repository
- Version stamped by date with HTML tags in the YYYYMMDD format

Figure 12.1 shows the process repository with process areas of interest to the software project manager so marked. I should be able to see all the versions (by date) on all process elements right up to the latest and greatest version — the tip. Figure 12.2 graphically shows the versions.

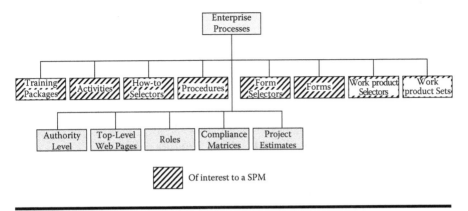

Figure 12.1 Process repository starting structure.

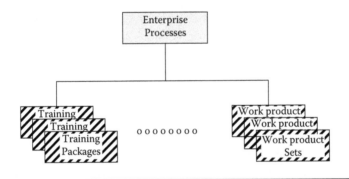

Figure 12.2 Structure to determine process basis candidates.

The project has one piece of data needed to extract all the process candidates as the process basis for this particular project. That one piece of data is the project start date (you could use the term *start of proposal*, because it's project specific, but, generally, the phrase *paid start date* is better). With that single date, you can scan all the files in the process repository and identify the versions whose dates are closest in time or equal to that start date. This provides your initial candidate list of processes pertinent to your project. Ideally that scanning effort is done via script programming. You can do it manually if you want.

As an example, if our project started on December 13, 2005, that date would be in the form 20051213 to comply with the YYYYMMDD format. Let's say we had this sampling of process versions in our process repository:

- "Design Down" activity version 20051101, version 20050716, and version 20050202
- "Update Integration Plan" activity version 20051217, version 20051207, and version 20050620
- "Inspection" how-selector version 20060108, version 20051210, and version 20050821
- "Inspection" procedure (San Diego) version 20060105, version 20051213, and version 20050825
- "Inspection" procedure (Dallas) version 20051209, version 20051208, and version 20050825
- "Build" procedure version 20050705, version 20050404, version 20050317, and version 20041118

A sweep through this subset process repository using 20051213 as a search field will yield these "hits:"

- "Design Down" activity version 20051101
- "Update Integration Plan" activity version 20051207
- "Inspection" how-selector version 20051210
- "Inspection" procedure (San Diego) version 20051213
- "Inspection" procedure (Dallas) version 20051209
- "Build" procedure version 20050705

You probably have noticed that one of these items was an exact hit on date. The others are all closest in time to that date. This method allows process improvements to go on by adding later and still later versions of any process element. It is the software project manager's prerogative to "step up" to a later version if he or she chooses once the project is underway. It is not reasonable to chase process improvements automatically. That kind of process volatility just causes havoc on any project.

You're not finished yet, however. In this subset, you will notice that I have two inspection procedures — one for San Diego and one for Dallas. If we are a San Diego project, you can delete the Dallas version of the inspection procedure from your list.

For process activities, you merely identify the closest- or equal-in-time activities to your project start date as your process basis. Typically, this goes in your PMP (project management plan). The activity part of your process basis is almost boilerplate stuff and should take a few minutes.

This is also true of training packages, how-selectors, work product selectors, form selectors, templates, inspection checklists, etc.

In the procedural how-to world, work product world, and form world, you have one more task to do to establish your process basis: select one (or more) from each selectable set. I mention "or more" because the software project manager may have a primary pick for one part of the life cycle and a secondary pick for another part of the life cycle. Additional training may be involved in that decision. Most of the time, one selection from each group is made. I feel that software quality assurance (SQA) has a definite role to play in validating those selections by a project manager. I have certainly seen some project managers select procedures based on an unprofessional attitude, (how much can I get away with) not on an analysis of what is appropriate for this project. At one company where I worked, they had one-person projects of writing demonstration software. A design review for that kind of project will be very informal and pertinent to that one-person effort. A fifty-person project's design review would be much more formal. You can't allow a project manager to pick the informal version for a fifty-person project just because it is easier. That's where SQA comes in as an enterprise "conscience."

When completed, the process lineup for this project is described in the PMP. As an aside, I am a proponent of physically placing the process basis descriptions in the project's developmental repository and referencing (or copying) that file from the PMP. The main process basis is in the project developmental repository, however. The placement in the repository makes it unambiguous for these users:

- You — the software project manager
- Project support team
- Developers
- SQA
- SCM (software configuration management)
- Customer
- Subcontractors

To all people working your project (in any capacity), the question, "what processes do I use?" is absolutely known:

- Developers know what how-to procedures, work products, forms, and training packages to use on this project.
- Quality knows what process elements are to be audited for this project.

■ Subcontractors know what they need as how-to alternatives for scheduled activities.
■ Customers know what processes you are using on their project.

Repositories

There are three repositories that need setting up at this time:

■ The project developmental repository
■ The project's sandbox
■ The project release repository*

At proposal time, we should have established the top-level structure of a proposal repository. This is the time to make that same repository the developmental repository. What we get coming into the setup phase is:

■ The top-level structure with project as a root node and proposal and system as subdirectories
■ Proposal area populated with proposal work products**

Because we are being paid for work now, we need to populate this repository with templates and placeholders as follows:

■ Under "Project:" Charge number template file, process basis file, all templates for deliverables, all known project-level work product templates or placeholders. This is a great place for the schedule itself.
■ Under "System:" All known system-level work product templates or placeholders.

The "we" part represents SCM. I certainly see a SQA role here to validate/check this file population. This is shown in Figure 12.3 and Figure 12.4.

---

* Some companies have a separate and distinct repository for releases whereas others handle this via the developmental repository and have meta-scripts related to important releases within that repository. For this book, I will assume a separate and distinct repository.

** Some work products may be starting files for execution — such as system design. These types of files should be placed under "system."

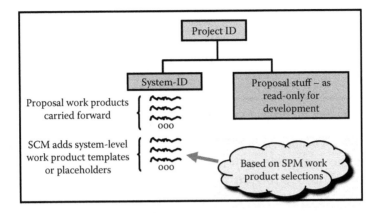

Figure 12.3 **Structure to add system-level placeholders and templates.**

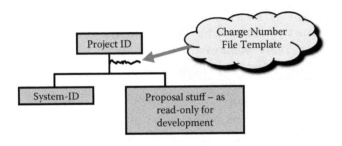

Figure 12.4 **Add project-level template for charge numbers.**

Templates and work product versions are based on the project's process basis file contents that were determined by the software project manager. There may be more than one version of a template and it's important to get the right one in that repository.

The SCM seeding of version 0 files is important for several reasons:

■ It establishes a set of work products to be processed.
■ It provides an instant view of what is not getting done; i.e., the original template/placeholder is still there.
■ It provides unambiguous get-started templates for development.
■ It allows process elements to always GET — even the first time.

Now let's turn our attention to the project's sandbox. I introduced this sandbox concept in Figures 6.5 and 6.6. At this time, we don't know the piece/part story, so we can't set up all the piece/part object names as subfolders to each activity. The piece/part story unfolds as

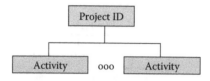

Figure 12.5 Set up project sandbox.

we execute "Design Down" activities at execution time. What we can set up is the root node with all the activity names as subfolders. This top-level sandbox structure is now established for all activities as a runtime working area. This is shown in Figure 12.5.

Finally, we set up a project release repository that will contain those matching sets of versioned work products that go together as a release package. Unlike the developmental repository, we also want to capture the following:

- The exact versions of the compilers that produced this code for reproducibility purposes
- Chip set versions (if applicable) if software is "burned on" any chip
- Exact build instructions
- Version descriptions
- Executable code modules
- Hardware versions (if applicable) on which the software resides
- Jumper cable settings if applicable
- Any others

Of these repositories, the developmental repository and the project's sandbox are the most critical to set up now. The release repository can be deferred until it's close to being needed.

Charge Numbers

In Chapter 8, I described the general concept behind both the WBS and the charge number to support this process-based SPM approach.

A project charge number is established at the time you go after it (after the bid decision). The establishment of a charge number is not delayed until the start of execution. Charges prior to the actual proposal should be nonproject and general in nature. If I can use the analogy of pregnancy, you establish a project at conception time, not at birth time. Conception time for a project is the start of the proposal phase. The reasons for this are quite simple:

■ Work is expended — even though you're not paid for it. You need to know what this is.

■ You need a basic charge number system early on to capture these project charges.

■ The SCM repository needs to be set up to jump-start execution from any work developed earlier.

■ You need valid company metrics on the cost of doing business when you don't get accepted for execution.

■ You execute process activities before execution as part of the overall life cycle. They need tracking.

General business development charges need to be extrapolated over all your projects if you really want to include those pre-proposal charges as part of overhead.

I recognize that because proposal charges and execution charges are mutually exclusive, you certainly have the option to have one charge number interpretation at proposal time to be replaced by another interpretation at execution time. I have not addressed proposal-time charge numbers in this book, but I hope you recognize that this overlay tactic could be used. To avoid this dual use of activities (pre-execution and execution), I strongly recommend that all your pre-execution activities have names different from those used at execution. Most are mutually exclusive, but some can show up in both places. For those, make a distinction between the pre-execution form of that activity and the execution form of that activity.

In this chapter, I will build on that information and show you what one such execution charge number may resemble. Figure 12.6 shows a top-level nine-digit charge number format.

The basic charge number structure is made up of three major elements:

■ The project identifier, shown as PP

■ The WBS — schedulable and nonschedulable sections

■ The rework counter

The WBS portion is further organized into two main chunks:

■ Activity numbered 00 followed by the nonschedulable aspects of the WBS

■ Activity identifications, numbered 01 through 99, followed by the schedulable aspects of the WBS

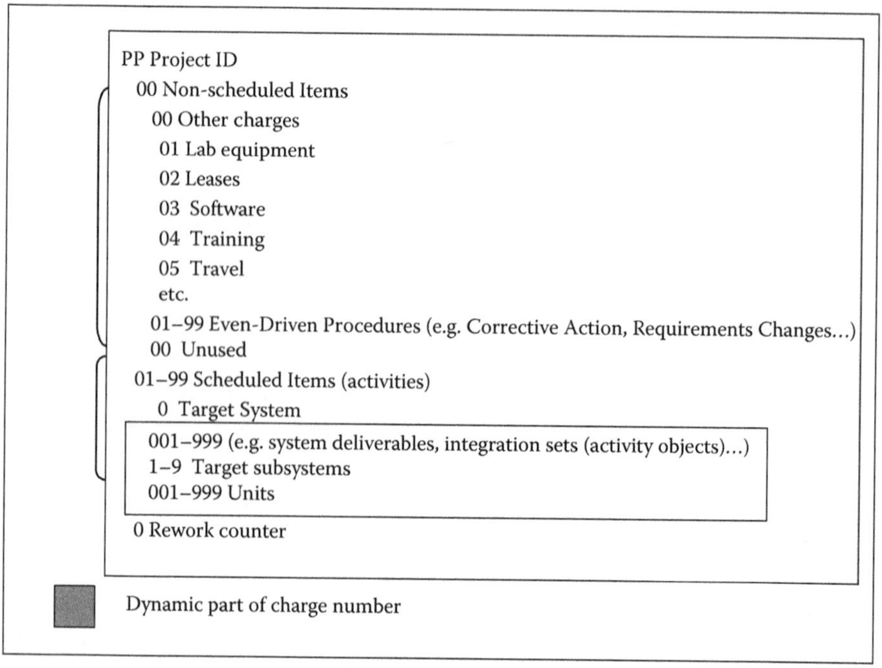

PP Project ID
  00 Non-scheduled Items
    00 Other charges
     01 Lab equipment
     02 Leases
     03 Software
     04 Training
     05 Travel
     etc.
    01–99 Even-Driven Procedures (e.g. Corrective Action, Requirements Changes...)
    00 Unused
  01–99 Scheduled Items (activities)
    0 Target System
     001–999 (e.g. system deliverables, integration sets (activity objects)...)
     1–9 Target subsystems
     001–999 Units
  0 Rework counter

▨ Dynamic part of charge number

Figure 12.6   Top-level nine-digit charge number format.

For companies with lots and lots of activities, this may be a three-digit front end rather than two.

The nonscheduled portion is further subdivided into two camps:

■ Other charges represented by 00, such as lab equipment, leases, software, training, travel, etc.
■ All the event-driven procedures represented by 01, ..., 99 in which work happens.

The scheduled portion is also subdivided into two camps:

■ System-level activities for all the system objects (such as deliverables) represented by 0. This captures work related to that object for any given activity.
■ All the subsystems in which work happens represented by 1, ..., 9.

The subsystem portion drills-down to yet another layer:

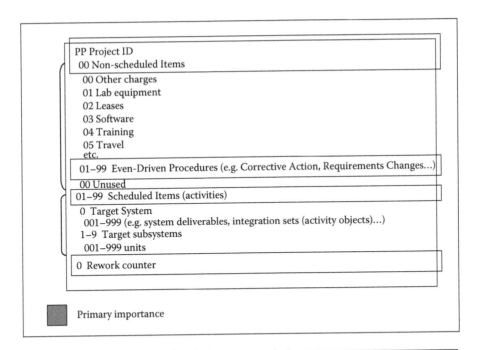

PP Project ID
00 Non-scheduled Items
  00 Other charges
  01 Lab equipment
  02 Leases
  03 Software
  04 Training
  05 Travel
  etc.
  01–99 Even-Driven Procedures (e.g. Corrective Action, Requirements Changes...)
  00 Unused
  01–99 Scheduled Items (activities)
  0 Target System
    001–999 (e.g. system deliverables, integration sets (activity objects)...)
  1–9 Target subsystems
    001–999 units
  0 Rework counter

  ▨ Primary importance

Figure 12.7   Process-based view of charge numbers.

- Subsystem-related objects represented by 000
- All the units within any given subsystem represented by 001, ..., 999.

In Figure 12.6, you'll notice a box around part of this charge number structure. It is that portion of the charge number that is dynamic. That part can be determined once the appropriate "Design Down" activities are executed in which we know the number of subsystems and units within those subsystems for sure.

This charge number form can provide two different views or perspectives using that charge number:

- The process-based view
- The piece/part-based view

The process-based view is shown in Figure 12.7.

You will notice that I have highlighted the parts of the charge number that provide that process viewpoint.

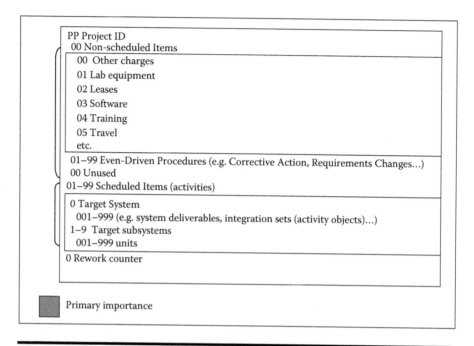

Figure 12.8   Piece/part view of charge numbers.

Figure 12.8 shows the same format but with a piece/part perspective highlighted for the reader. This duality meaning of charge numbers with one orientation to piece/part objects provides metrics data such as these:

■ Summary of all activities (tasks) related to a particular activity object (e.g., all charges related to subsystem A)
■ Summary of all event-driven procedures related to a particular activity object (e.g., all charges related to system X)

The piece/part view is an inverted process view of any charge number.

Now, I hope you can see that the target portion of any charge number comes from two places:

■ The schedule and "Design Down" execution provides the activity/activity object part of this.
■ Accounting provides the wrapper charge number part of this.

This division is shown graphically in Figure 12.9. This figure may be a little misleading because I have not included reworked activity costs.

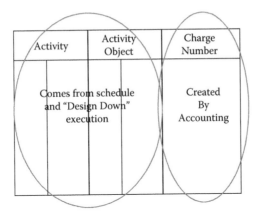

Figure 12.9   Target portion of charge number.

Let's turn our attention to rework. Most companies have no real grasp of the real cost of rework. With this alignment of charge numbers to process activities to schedule tasks, you can now directly address the cost of rework.

I recommend you leave a single digit at the end of your charge number as the rework indicator. The number 0 indicates first time through (or no rework) whereas 1 through 9 indicates a rework counter.

You are marching along your schedule, when your customer makes some serious changes to your requirements. You are past design and have started some implementation. You need to do an impact analysis on those requirements changes to determine what needs reworking based on where you are in the life cycle; you need to "prune" some schedule tree branches for rework based on redesigns that need doing, and so forth You prune all the schedule tasks and move them forward in the schedule and either start with 1 at the end of the charge number or add 1 to what you have (with a cycle of 9). Any charge number with anything but a 0 at the end is a rework item. How's that for utter simplicity in getting a handle on actual rework costs! The rework part of the charge number comes directly from the project schedule. I hope the reader will notice that a rework counter of 3 indicates you've done this three times.

Planning Schedule

The big ticket item when setting up any software planning project at execution time is to establish all schedule line items such that they truly reflect work to be done. You never want anything on that planning schedule that can cause you grief when attempting to track work progress.

In my mind, the planning schedule is made up of two threads of information:

- Contractual/management thread
- Target-system thread

The only facts you know for sure are the contractual elements needed in your planning schedule. These include, among others, the following:

- Deliverables, including versions or updates of each
- Major reviews needed
- Periodic technical update meetings

This contractual thread should be known and can be laid out on a schedule. You might need some minor tweaking for placement but all the elements should be accounted for. The proposal schedule would have included these contractual items most likely as feedback items.

From a target-system perspective, no execution-time designs have been done to even give you a clue about the nature and organization of those target-system-related schedule tasks. At best, you have a summary schedule reflecting an estimated system piece/part story.

The question becomes this: "how much of the proposal schedule (related to the target system) is salvageable as an execution planning schedule?" If you had used the process repository as an estimation tool, you would have laid out the estimated pieces/parts according to process direction for your proposal. Figure 12.10 shows the relationship of process phase process activity diagram (PAD) inputs to create that proposal schedule.

In Figure 12.10, I showed six phases as examples that were used as inputs into creating that proposal schedule. Your life cycle may differ from what I have shown. We know right now that most of the back end of this is absolutely bogus as a planning schedule because it reflects estimations for everything.

To create that initial planning schedule related to the target-system thread, we have a basic choice of either of the following:

- Cut back (or cull) known fictitious chunks of that proposal schedule that are to be our initial planning schedule
- Create that initial planning schedule using life-cycle process guidance

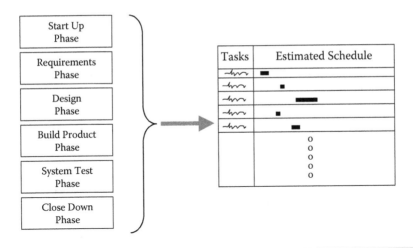

Figure 12.10   Proposal-time execution schedule basis.

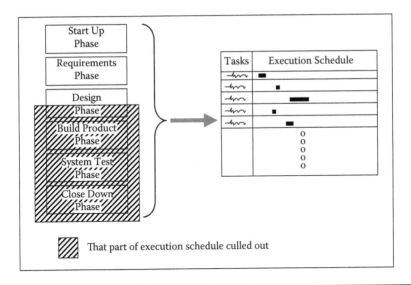

Figure 12.11   Cull that execution schedule basis.

Figure 12.11 shows the former whereas Figure 12.12 shows the latter.

The first figure (Figure 12.11) graphically shows what needs to be dropped or culled from the original estimation schedule to create the target-system thread. The only facts we know for sure are all the activities (with their predecessor/successor relationships) up to and

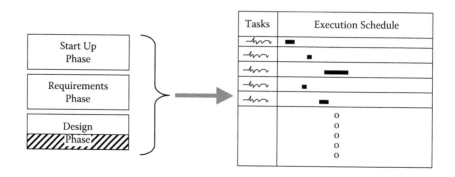

Figure 12.12   Create initial execution schedule.

including the system-level design. After that, we consider everything else as fiction. Because schedule tasking comes totally from activity roadmaps inside phase PADs, we know exactly what tasks are going to be needed, and in what order, up to the top-level system design. That becomes our initial planning schedule related to the target system. If you had not used this process roadmap for estimation, Figure 12.12 shows you a similar story, but you need to build your planning schedule directly from your process PADs, as shown.

At this point, our initial planning schedule should have an accurate depiction of the following:

- All contractual schedule tasks/events
- All target-system schedule tasks up to and including the system-level design

We can fill in all the activity objects because they are all either "project" or "system." What we don't have (and need to add) are these:

- Activity lead name assignments per schedule task/event
- Calendar-based initial planning schedule converted from a pure duration in the proposal time

There is a possibility that some of our contractual line items (tasks/events) may have to be placeholders at the bottom of the schedule until we can map them properly as our visibility improves on the unfolding schedule.

We now have a complete initial planning schedule that has a high degree of correctness for project execution and tracking. The target-system part of this schedule is totally blank at this time after "Design

Down (system)." I can just tell that traditional software project managers are going to cringe about that. I would rather have nothing on this schedule to be used for tracking than a fantasyland approach of putting tasks on the schedule with a hope that they reflect reality. I've experienced too many bloodbaths over this very circumstance when reality met fantasy on a schedule.

Chapter 13

Planning up to Design

Introduction

There is an interesting phenomenon that factors into your execution-time planning schedule, which includes the following:

- You absolutely know all the contract-related tasks/events. You may not know where they all fit at this point in time.
- You only know target-system-related tasks up to and including system design. After that, you haven't a clue what goes on a schedule for planning purposes because the actual design has not occurred yet.

All the work you have done during the pre-execution segment, culminating in getting a proposal out, was estimated using the AVG (average) factors. This is because pre-execution work is all nonpaid work and is thus overhead. All the projected execution-time activities rolled up for the customer use the loaded average factor or L-AVG. These same activities up to and including the system-level "Design Down" from your proposal estimations can now be the initial planning schedule, using the same L-AVG estimations when we work these activities (or tasks).

Contract Schedule Items Planning

For the contract schedule items, I recommend placing them all on your schedule as schedule line items — even if they are put at the bottom as mind-jogger items for later placement. The schedule is a great place to store these contract schedule items so that you don't forget any. Fixed periodic contract items can be placed there now but other contract tasks/events may have successor relationships to target schedule items that are not there yet.

Target-System Schedule Items Planning

For the target-system schedule items up to and including system design, you have two marvelous clues as to what should go there; these are the following:

- The target-system proposal schedule itself — if you used the process basis for estimation
- The process life cycle process activity diagrams (PADs) relevant to getting you up to system design

Figure 13.1 shows those proposal-phase target-system activities and their relationship to your initial planning schedule for execution. Figure 13.2 shows what actual phase PADs are included in that transfer. An interesting thing to note about Figure 13.2 is that project setup is being done right then, i.e., the steps I'm talking about in this book are the very guidance steps executed by the software project manager and members of his or her role partner team.

You might have done some activities totally at proposal time (such as normalizing requirements) and thus don't need to do them again at execution time. Other activities (such as clarifying requirements) may have been partially done at proposal time but need to be finished at execution time. For that scenario, you'll have a "P-Clarify Requirements" activity at proposal time and a "Clarify Requirements" at execution time. This separation clearly tells the practitioner that the former is done prior to execution, as part of the proposal effort, whereas the latter is done after contract award during the execution segment.

Figure 13.3 shows a possible requirements-phase PAD that we know needs to show up on the initial planning schedule.

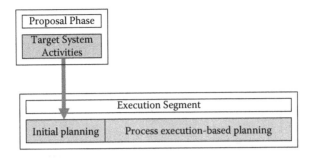

Figure 13.1   Proposal connection to initial planning schedule.

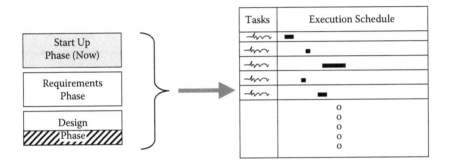

Figure 13.2   Actual phase PADs involved in the initial planning schedule.

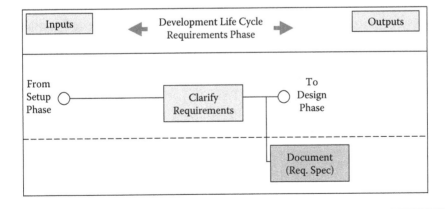

Figure 13.3   Possible "Requirements Phase" PAD.

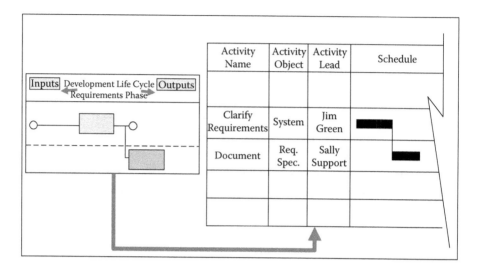

Figure 13.4 Requirements PAD converted to a schedule.

Observe that we show a single mainline activity called "Clarify Requirements" in one swim plane and we have one support-type activity in the other swim lane. If we had done partial requirements clarifications at proposal time, there would have been a "P-Clarify Requirements" activity within the proposal-phase PAD. Also observe that if you have the need to create a real document called a "Requirements Specification," it has a predecessor connection to the "Clarify Requirements" activity; i.e., we don't do it until the predecessor activity is "done." If you don't have a need to create a real document, you merely don't do that activity. Remember, each activity is selectable as an atomic element. If this was your process-phase PAD, you have all the guidance you need to put that part of the planning schedule together. Figure 13.4 shows the planning schedule that was directly derived from the process-phase PAD.

Let's turn our attention now to bringing the planning schedule up to system design. Figure 13.5 shows a possible design-phase PAD from the process world.

There are some points to be made about this figure, which are as follows:

■ Quite often, there is a large time gap between any proposal submission and the contract award. There is a high probability that the folks that worked on the proposal are not the same group that will be working the project. It is safe to assume that the

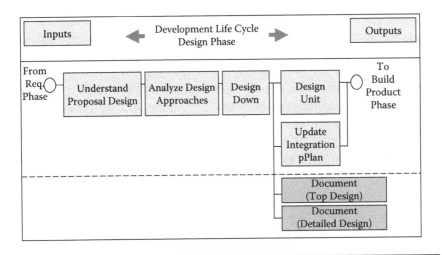

Figure 13.5   Possible "Design Phase" PAD.

proposal-time team had to understand the requirements, etc., to come up with a proposed design. This new team may not be up to speed on the proposed design at all, and they will need to be.

■ Again, I would assume that the proposal-time team looked at different design approaches before settling on the proposed design. If that is true, you probably don't want to analyze design approaches again. That tells me that you will want to skip the analyze design approaches activity at execution time. That particular activity exists in case you really do need to analyze design approaches at execution time.

■ At proposal time, there would have been a gross (or rough) design effort done at the system level. A "P-Design Down" would have been done in the proposal phase. This "Design Down" is a known activity that we definitely need in the initial planning schedule at execution time.

■ If there is a contractual need for a top-level design document, we can place that support activity on the initial planning schedule immediately. If a design document is not called for, we don't need to do this support activity (task).

■ All the other parts of this phase PAD are not needed just yet for our initial planning schedule. We have to wait for the "Design Down (system)" task to be executed to really know the subsystem story. We also have to wait for each "Design Down (subsystem)" task to be executed to really know the unit story for that subsystem.

At this point, we have completed our initial planning schedule and know for sure that each and every schedule task represents real work to be done and can be tracked on a 1:1 basis with the planning schedule. We also know that each schedule task (or activity instance) has estimated durations, work units, manpower numbers, etc., based on the "L-AVG" associated with each of those activity types. We also know that when we get to activity tracking, we have a built-in maximum (MAX) estimate that can be used as a trigger for any variance reporting for your earned value system.

Chapter 14

Planning after Design

Introduction

This is by far the potential "choke point" for planning if not done correctly. Conversely, it virtually guarantees a smooth planning schedule for tracking purposes if done correctly. This process-based software project management approach does not allow planning tasks on a schedule unless they are known for sure. This level of knowingness has to come directly from the execution of key tasks (such as "Design Down" and "Update Integration Plan" tasks) coupled with prompt action by you as software project manager and your role partners. This is the one area in which this process approach is not very forgiving if you and your team don't act promptly.

There will be traditional software project managers that get really nervous about all this right now. After all, up to top-level design, you have almost nothing on your planning schedule; after top-level design and integration plan are done, you have the whole works!

Planning "Design Down (System)"

I intend to walk you through this planning drill. Let's start back at the design-phase process activity diagram (PAD) from the process repository. We want to convert that PAD representation of activities onto our project schedule. This is shown in Figure 14.1.

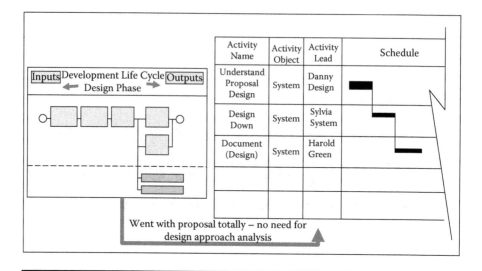

Figure 14.1   Design-phase PAD mapped onto schedule.

At execution time, I have a design team different from proposal time. I need the design team to understand the proposal design. I place that first activity on my planning schedule and add the activity object (the system name) and the proposed activity lead's name.

I will accept the proposal-time design approach so there is no need for the "analyze design approaches" activity to be placed on the schedule. Because activities are atomic elements and are selectable, I can do this.

I know for sure that I can place the "Design Down (system)" and "Document (system)" activities on the schedule. Because of the predecessor/successor relationships shown on the phase PAD, I know that I can place the "Design Down (system)" after the "Understand Proposal Design" task. I also know that I can attach the "Document" type of activity after the "Design Down" task. Beyond that, I cannot put anything more onto the schedule because we haven't executed that top-level design yet.

To take you through a real-world scenario, I am going to assume the following results of design activities at the system and subsystem levels:

■ The target system is made up of two subsystems: subsystem A and subsystem B.
■ Subsystem A is made up of 100 units:
  – Units 1–10 are reused units that need additional "tweaking."
  – Units 11–25 are reused units that can be used as is.

- Units 26–45 need to be designed and are considered critical. They require unit testing beyond code inspections.
- Units 46–100 need to be designed and do not need unit testing, but just code inspections.
■ Subsystem B is made up of 50 units:
- Units 1–10 need to be designed and are considered critical. They require unit testing beyond code inspections.
- Units 11–50 need to be designed and do not need unit testing, but just code inspections.

I will later describe my assumptions as a result of "Update Integration Plan" activity executions. For now, we'll go with the earlier assumptions.

The "Design Down (system)" activity is the top-level system design that does a design down to the subsystem level. After executing the "Design Down (system)" task on the project schedule, the design calls out that there are two subsystems: subsystem A and subsystem B.

Recall that the END high-level step of the "Design Down" activity (and thus schedule task) has a crucial role to play for project planning. You as software project manager and your role partners are notified. Actions by each are as follows:

Software project manager:
■ You need two more "Design Down" tasks on the project schedule: one called "Design Down (subsystem A)" and the other called "Design Down (subsystem B)" in which the subsystem names are the activity objects.
■ You know that these two new tasks have the "Design Down (system)" task as the predecessor task.
■ After each "Design Down (subsystem)," you could certainly update your detailed design document.
■ You need two "Update Integration Plan tasks" on the project schedule: one called "Update Integration Plan (subsystem A)" and the other called "Update Integration Plan (subsystem B)" in which the subsystem names are the activity objects. These are needed because you have now designed down to the lowest-level "leaf" elements — the units.
■ The "Update Integration Plan (subsystem A)" task has the "Design Down (subsystem A)" task as the predecessor task.
■ The "Update Integration Plan (subsystem B)" task has the "Design Down (subsystem B)" task as the predecessor task. Figure 14.2 shows these.

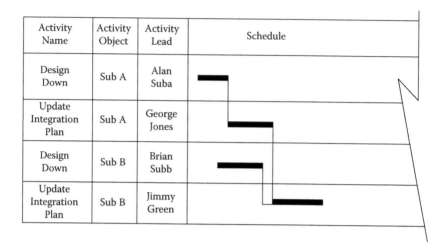

Activity Name	Activity Object	Activity Lead	Schedule
Design Down	Sub A	Alan Suba	
Update Integration Plan	Sub A	George Jones	
Design Down	Sub B	Brian Subb	
Update Integration Plan	Sub B	Jimmy Green	

Figure 14.2   Schedule after system-level "Design Down" execution.

- You know that the respective activity-type-loaded estimations (duration) using the L-AVG factors will be used for task durations on the project schedule.
- Get together with engineering for activity lead determination and manpower assignments for the preceding new tasks.
- Optionally, fill in the charge number for each task after accounting has determined that number.*

Software configuration management (SCM):

- SCM knows for sure that they need two more subfolders under the system folder in the developmental repository, one for each subsystem.
- SCM knows that the developmental repository subfolders are "Subsystem A" and "Subsystem B" in particular. See Figure 14.3.
- SCM knows to populate each subfolder with all the known subsystem templates or placeholders needed during development.
- SCM knows for sure to add both these subfolders named earlier to all the activity folders (that have the potential for a generic subsystem object) in the project's sandbox. For example, under "Design Down" folder in the project's sandbox,

---

* In one implementation, it was found that actually storing the charge number with the task was beneficial. That is your choice to make.

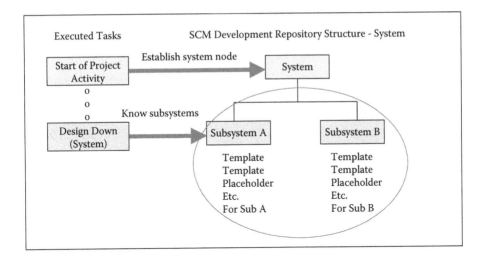

Figure 14.3 SCM action on system-level "Design Down" execution.

you would add "Subsystem A" and "Subsystem B" to the existing "System" subfolder. After SCM action, "Design Down" would now have three subfolders against the one before.

Accounting:
- Accounting now knows that there are two subsystems named A and B.
- Accounting can now assign charge number codes for each subsystem. See Figure 14.4.
- Accounting can now make sure the charge number file (at the project level in the project's developmental repository) has the charge number mapping to the symbolic piece/part names.

Software quality assurance (SQA):
- SQA can now verify the structure and initial population of the developmental repository set up by SCM.
- SQA can now verify the structure of the project's sandbox set up by SCM.
- SQA can now verify the contents of the charge number file set up by Accounting.
- SQA can now possibly verify the added schedule tasks and their connectivity to other tasks set up by the software project manager.

```
PP Project ID
   00 Non-scheduled Items
      00 Other charges
         01 Lab equipment
         02 Leases
         03 Software
         04 Training
         05 Travel
         etc.
      01–99 Even-Driven Procedures (e.g. Corrective Action, Requirements Changes…)
      00 Unused
   01–99 Scheduled Items (activities)
      0  Target System
         001–nnn (system deliverables should have been assigned)
            1 Subsystem A
            2 Subsystem B
         000 Unassigned units
   0 Rework counter
```

Figure 14.4   Charge number after system-level "Design Down" execution.

Planning "Design Down (Subsystem A)"

The "Design Down (subsystem A)" activity is the next-level design that does a design down to the unit level. After executing the "Design Down (subsystem A)" task on the project schedule, the design calls out that there are 100 units. The big difference between this "Design Down" and the system-level "Design Down" is that the decomposed designed elements are units or lowest-leaf elements for design. For this task, I ask the developers to not only identify the decomposed elements or units but add the following attributes to each unit:

- Does it need designing?
- Is it a reused unit?
- Does it need coding (whether new or reuse tweaking)?
- Does it need to be unit tested (or does a code inspection suffice)?

These attributes are critical to the software project manager for this process-based approach, because they provide an exact layout of tasks per unit. I also ask the developers to give their best shot as to which subset of those units should be done early. Software engineering knows this. The early-up units provide the software project manager with

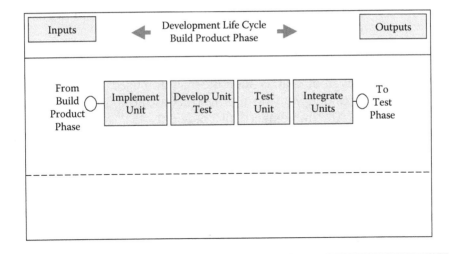

Figure 14.5   Possible "Build Product" phase PAD.

guidance on what needs to go on the schedule early — even before any integration plan is done that can possibly validate this. The software project manager cannot wait for the integration plan to be done to lay out planned work to be done on the project schedule.

Just as before, the END high-level step of the "Design Down" activity (and thus schedule task) has a crucial role to play for project planning. You (as software project manager) and your role partners are notified. Actions by each are as follows:

Software project manager:
- ■ You need 100 units to be accounted for on the project schedule in which the actual unit filenames are the activity objects.
- ■ You know what the early-up units are for scheduling.
- ■ You know what pattern of unit activities are appropriate for each unit based on the unit attributes mentioned earlier. Figure 14.5 shows a possible "Build Product" phase PAD showing these process activities. Let's go through some of these:
  - – Any unit to be designed, coded, and tested needs the following:
    - • A "Design Unit" task
    - • An "Implement Unit" task
    - • A "Develop Unit Test" task
    - • A "Test Unit" task

- Any unit to be designed, coded but not tested needs the following:
  - A "Design Unit" task
  - An "Implement Unit" task
- Any unit that is identified as a reused unit but needs tweaking with no unit test needs the following:
  - An "Implement Unit" task only
- Any unit that is identified as a reused unit but can be used as is with no unit test needs the following:
  - <Nothing> note: Still suggest an explicit line item for this unit to show it was not just a forgotten unit — even if it's a null entry
- Any unit that is identified as a reused unit but needs tweaking and requires a unit test needs the following:
  - An "Implement Unit" task
  - A "Develop Unit test" task
  - A "Test Unit" task

■ You know which of the preceding patterns to use for the early-up units identified by engineering.

■ You know that the respective activity-type loaded estimations (duration) using the L-AVG factors will be used for task durations on the project schedule for all unit-based activities.

■ Get together with engineering for activity lead determination and manpower assignments for the new tasks mentioned earlier.

■ As before, you could fill in the charge number for each task after accounting has determined it.

SCM:

■ SCM knows for sure that they need 100 more subfolders under the "Subsystem A" folder in the developmental repository — one for each unit.

■ SCM knows that the filenames of each and every unit, in particular, filenames prior to file extensions, are used as the subfolder names.

■ SCM knows to populate each subfolder with all the known unit templates or placeholders needed during development if applicable.

■ SCM knows for sure to add the 100 subfolders named earlier to all the activity folders (that have the potential for a generic unit object) in the project's sandbox. For example, under the "Design Unit" folder in the project's sandbox, you would add all 100 unit names as subfolders.

```
PP Project ID
  00 Non-scheduled Items
     00 Other charges
        01 Lab equipment
        02 Leases
        03 Software
        04 Training
        05 Travel
        etc.
     01–99 Even-Driven Procedures (e.g. Corrective Action, Requirements Changes...)
     00 Unused
  01–99 Scheduled Items (activities)
     0 Target System
        001-nnn (system deliverables should have been assigned)
        1 Subsystem A
          001–100 units (101.999 unassigned)
        2 Subsystem B
        000 Unassigned units
     0 Rework counter
```

Figure 14.6   Charge number after "Design Down (subsystem A)" execution.

Accounting:

- Accounting now knows that there are 100 units in subsystem A.
- Accounting can now assign charge number codes for each unit. See Figure 14.6.
- Accounting can now make sure the charge number file (at the project level in the project's developmental repository) has the charge number mapping to the symbolic unit names.

SQA:

- SQA can now verify the structure and initial population of the developmental repository at the unit level (for subsystem A) set up by SCM.
- SQA can now verify the structure of the project's sandbox set up by SCM related to units in subsystem A.
- SQA can now verify the contents of the charge number file set up by Accounting.
- SQA can now possibly verify the added schedule tasks and their connectivity to other tasks set up by the SPM.

Planning "Update Integration Plan (Subsystem A)"

Back in Figure 14.2, I showed this activity being executed after the "Design Down (subsystem A)." On the initial execution of this activity, the version of the integration plan that we're updating is the version 0 template only at this point in time.

This is a key task for the software project manager. The END high-level step is used to notify the software project manager that an integration plan has been updated. The END does not reflect that this is the final update of the integration plan. The software project manager needs the project schedule to make that call. This task is important to the project manager because it takes the set of designed units from the "Design Down (subsystem A)" and provides an ordering for the project schedule. The "Design Down" by itself just identifies the decomposed pieces/parts and provides a get-started hint about which units should be done early.

The information we have is that subsystem A has 100 units, some of which are totally reused, some are reused with some modifications, and some are to be developed from scratch. The development team executing this particular activity has the following responsibilities:

- Define integration sets of units.
- Define an integration ordering of those sets.*

For illustration purposes, I'm going to assume the following:

- Integration Set 1A = units 1–40
- Integration Set 2A = units 41–50
- Integration Set 3A = units 51–80
- Integration Set 4A = units 81–100

Based on this first (incomplete) update of the integration plan, the software project manager knows the following:

- Units 1–40 need to be done early.
- Units 41–50 need to be done after units 1–40.
- Units 51–80 need to be done after units 41–50.
- Units 81–100 need to be done after units 51–80.

---

* Because this is the first subsystem, we don't have other sets from any other subsystem to incorporate at this time.

The actual integration ordering may change on the next (final) update of the integration plan. Even with this partial information, the software project manager can do intelligent ordering of the unit activities such that they align with the integration planning. Looking at the unit lineup already mentioned, the project manager knows that unit 93 can be significantly deferred from unit 23 for schedule planning. The project manager also knows that units 1–40 all need to be "done" before you can ever have any kind of integration testing.

Planning "Design Down (Subsystem B)"

Similar to the "Design Down (subsystem A)" activity, the "Design Down (subsystem B)" is another second-level design that does a design down to the unit level. After executing the "Design Down (subsystem B)" task on the project schedule, the design calls out that there are 50 units. Similar to the subsystem A design, this design also asks the developers for unit-related attributes, etc.

As before, the END high-level step of this "Design Down" activity (and thus schedule task) has a crucial role to play for project planning. You (as software project manager) and your role partners are again notified. Actions by each are as follows:

Software project manager:
- You need 50 units to be accounted for on the project schedule in which the actual unit filenames are the activity objects.
- You know what the early-up units (related to subsystem B) are for scheduling.
- You know what pattern of unit activities are appropriate for each unit (from subsystem B) based on the unit attributes supplied by engineering. This is what we know for sure:
  - Units 1–10 are to be designed, coded, and tested. They need this pattern:
    - A "Design Unit" task
    - An "Implement Unit" task
    - A "Develop Unit Test" task
    - A "Test Unit" task
  - Units 11–50 are to be designed and coded but not tested. They need the following:
    - A "Design Unit" task
    - An "Implement Unit" task

- You know which of these patterns to use for the early-up units identified by engineering.
- You know that the respective activity-type-loaded estimations (duration) using the L-AVG factors will be used for task durations on the project schedule for all unit-based activities.
- Get together with engineering for activity lead determination and manpower assignments for the new tasks mentioned earlier.
- As before, you could fill in the charge number for each task after accounting has determined it.

SCM:

- SCM knows for sure that they need 50 more subfolders under the "Subsystem B" folder in the developmental repository — one for each unit.
- SCM knows that the filenames of each and every unit, in particular, filenames prior to file extensions, are used as the subfolder names.
- SCM knows to populate each subfolder with all the known unit templates or placeholders needed during development if applicable.
- SCM knows for sure to add 50 subfolders named earlier to all the activity folders (that have the potential for a generic unit object) in the project's sandbox. For example, under "Implement Unit" folder in the project's sandbox, you would add all 50 unit names as subfolders.

Accounting:

- Accounting now knows that there are 50 units in subsystem B.
- Accounting can now assign charge number codes for each unit. See Figure 14.7.
- Accounting can now make sure the charge number file (at the project level in the project's developmental repository) has the charge number mapping to the symbolic unit names.

SQA:

- SQA can now verify the structure and initial population of the developmental repository at the unit level (for subsystem B) set up by SCM.
- SQA can now verify the structure of the project's sandbox set up by SCM related to units in subsystem B.

```
PP Project ID
   00 Non-scheduled Items
      00 Other charges
         01 Lab equipment
         02 Leases
         03 Software
         04 Training
         05 Travel
         etc.
      01–99 Even-Driven Procedures (e.g. Corrective Action, Requirements Changes...)
      00  Unused
   01–99 Scheduled Items (activities)
      0  Target System
         001-nnn (system deliverables should have been assigned)
      1 Subsystem A
         001–100 units (101.999 unassigned)
      2 Subsystem B
         001–050 units (051.999 unassigned)
   0 Rework counter
```

Figure 14.7   Charge number after "Design Down (subsystem B)" execution.

- SQA can now verify the contents of the charge number file set up by Accounting.
- SQA can now possibly verify the added schedule tasks and their connectivity to other tasks set up by the software project manager.

Planning "Update Integration Plan (Subsystem B)"

Referring back to Figure 14.2 again, I showed the execution of this activity after the "Design Down (subsystem B)" and after "Update Integration Plan (subsystem A)." On execution of this activity, the integration plan being updated was the result of subsystem A's integration planning.

As before, the END high-level step is used to notify the software project manager that an integration plan has been updated. The difference here is that this update contains the final integration plan for schedule planning by the project manager.

The information we have is that subsystem B has 50 units. The development team executing this particular activity has the following responsibilities:

- Define integration sets of units from subsystem B.
- Define an integration ordering of those units.
- Merge the integration sets from the previous update (from subsystem A) to form a comprehensive integration plan.

For illustration purposes, I'm going to assume the following:

- Integration Set 1B = units 1–35
- Integration Set 2B = units 36–50

Based on the merging of integration sets, a comprehensive integration plan is notified to the software project manager:

- Integration set A = Integration set 1A
- Integration set B = Integration set A + Integration set 1B
- Integration set C = Integration set B + Integration sets 2A and 3A
- Integration set D = Integration set C + Integration set 2B
- Integration set E = Integration set D + Integration set 4A

I just used the single-alpha designation for activity sets used as objects when actually performing integration testing.

The software project manager knows the following schedule information for sure:

- There will be five instances of the "Integrate Units" activity on the project schedule.
- The ordering of those five integrations.
- Units 1–40 from subsystem A are the earliest scheduled units because those units are needed for integration set 1A.
- Units 1–35 from subsystem B are next because those units are needed for integration set 1B.
- Units 41–80 from subsystem A are next because those units are needed for integration sets 2A and 3A.
- Units 36–50 from subsystem B are next because those units are needed for integration set 2B.
- Units 81–100 from subsystem A are last because those units are needed for integration set 4A.

In addition, for each unit, the project manager knows exactly what activity threads are needed per activity to feed into each integration execution. This information came from engineering's "Design Down" activities on subsystem A and subsystem B. This is summarized in Table 14.1 and Table 14.2.

Table 14.1   Subsystem A

Units	Design Unit	Implement Unit	Develop Unit Test	Test Unit
1–10	No	Yes	No	No
11–25	No	No	No	No
26–40	Yes	Yes	Yes	Yes
41–45	Yes	Yes	Yes	Yes
46–80	Yes	Yes	No	No
81–100	Yes	Yes	No	No

Table 14.2   Subsystem B

Units	Design Unit	Implement Unit	Develop Unit Test	Test Unit
1–10	No	Yes	Yes	Yes
11–35	Yes	Yes	No	No
36–50	Yes	Yes	No	No

I leave it to the reader to complete the planning schedule with the "System Test" phase PAD. I am reluctant to spell this out because each company has a very different way of doing system testing. I have seen huge differences between the government contracting world and commercial companies in this area. At two commercial companies I worked for, they had different types of system testing that started off with a basic sanity test composed of some basic functions (to see if they worked first), regression testing, and, finally, a full system test.

I do maintain that once the "Design Down" and "Update Integration Plan" tasks are executed, the software project manager can lay out the entire planning schedule with a high certainty that the plan matches reality. You should never use the words "always" and "never" — so it is possible (although it is a slim possibility) that the software project manager might have to make some minor adjustments to this planning schedule.

The biggest impact on this planning schedule exists when requirements change during project execution and portions of the planning schedule need to be cut and moved on the schedule to accommodate rework. When that happens, the software project manager also changes the charge numbers of the reworked tasks to include the rework counter at the end of that charge number. Even then, the planned work should exactly match the proposed work.

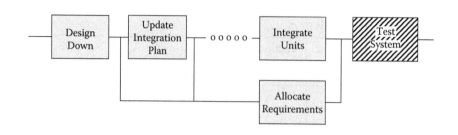

Figure 14.8   Consider separate "Allocate Requirements" to shorten life cycle.

Other Planning Considerations

For many years, I pushed for the notion that allocating requirements was an integral part of the "Design Down" type of activity. Using this process model, that notion would be implemented as a high-level step called "Allocate Requirements" within any "Design Down" activity. Being a high-level step ensures that it gets done. I was only partially correct. It is certainly true that a major result of any "Design Down" is to identify all the decomposed design pieces/parts of the target scope of that design. The "Design Down" on a system identifies all the subsystems. The "Design Down" on any subsystem identifies all the units within that subsystem. The flaw in my position was that you want to allocate requirements at the system–subsystem level, but you don't want to allocate requirements on the subsystem–unit level. The process model is very clear about not putting in high-level steps within any activity that can be optional. That's a big no-no. Allocating require-ments to pieces/parts of a system can be very onerous, costly, and time consuming if you allocate down to too low a level of detail, such as the unit level. Also, in practical terms, software engineers create units for all kinds of reasons including common functions, support units, etc. It's very difficult (if not impossible) to allocate down to that granularity for those reasons.

Why am I bringing this up? What has this got to do with SPM? It turns out it has a lot to do with SPM and can be instrumental in significantly shortening your overall life cycle and shortening your system test time. I now refer you to Figure 14.8.

A better way of doing this is to have a separate activity called "Allocate Requirements" that has a successor relationship to both the following:

- The "Design Down" activity
- The "Update Integration Plan" activity

The "Design Down" connection allows the software project manager to place the "Allocate Requirements" on a project schedule after the "Design Down (system)" task; but don't do this after a "Design Down (subsystem)" type of task. This way, you allocate requirements down to the subsystem level with that connectivity, but not at the unit level.

Let me refresh your memory about what the "Update Integration Plan" task does. A major result of this task execution is that groups of units are organized into integration sets. It is the integration set that gets merged onto an ever-widening base — also of integration sets. The point here is that we have created an entity that is not as high as a subsystem and not as low as a unit. Every time we execute an "Update Integration Plan," we have more visibility on the following:

- The number of integration sets
- The makeup of each integration set (i.e., the specific units)
- The integration ordering

From an "Allocate Requirements" perspective, we can allocate subsystem requirements to these higher-level chunks called integration sets. The burning question is why do this at all? What's in it for me?

This subsystem integration set allocation can be done totally in parallel with all your early unit-level implementation tasks right through to (and including) the first "Integrate Units" task. You don't need that allocation until after the first "Integrate Units" task is done. With that allocation, you have totally aligned your requirements with your integration efforts. What this means is that you can do an engineering integration immediately followed by a partial system test. Integration testing is an engineering function whose focus is on whether the designed pieces all fit together. System testing has a requirements focus to make sure that the customer needs (requirements) are met. When you allocate requirements to the integration sets, you can spawn incremental system testing intelligently by passing the requirements involved with this partial system test. I can't tell you how many times I have seen engineering throw something over the wall to system test with a curt "test this." The lack of qualification regarding test requirements causes all kinds of wasted system test time, countless error reports, and engineering/test thrashing. We want to avoid all this. This process model approach always calls upon a system test task to pass on "requirements under test." The testers know what not to do; they don't waste time doing nonsensical stuff. You can get a huge start on system testing connected directly to your integration tasking on your schedule. By the time you're at the final integration, most of your system testing is complete. That is why allocating requirements to integration sets is so important to any software project manager who is really serious about shortening the test time. I even advocate having a system testing role presence (along with engineering) in the "Update Integration Plan" task to make sure that the test team has a direct say about the integration sets. By having that presence, you can also have a huge start on your system test planning based on integration planning well before when you really need it.

You may have noticed that I shaded the "Test System" activity. That was done on purpose. Some companies do not have a single "flavor" of system testing but have procedures such as the following:

- A very basic test (sometimes called a *sanity* test) to make sure the new software under test still does some basic functions
- Regression testing to make sure the new software has not broken anything that was tested before
- A full system test to make sure that all the customer needs (requirements) are met
- An operational test that moves out of the lab environment to the real-world environment in which the software is supposed to perform

Just showing a single activity called *test system* may indeed be several activities noted earlier.

If you had that kind of system test breakdown, the software project manager would probably place that single activity after the first integration completion because of the following:

- You may not have enough basic functionality to do a sanity test.
- You have no regression testing because this is the first-up system test task.

On subsequent integrations, these two additional activities would show up on your project schedule. The sanity test is a judgment call on the point at which you have enough to perform some basic functions. Subsequent integrations would always need regression testing. The final integration execution would invoke all four activities, the fourth activity being the operational test. I am somewhat reluctant to be too specific here because every company does have a different suite of activities involved in system testing. I did want to show one possibility, however, in case you need that type of information where you work.

I hope I have shown in the preceding text that allocating requirements down to the integration sets can allow you to do partial system testing while engineering development is still progressing. This SPM action can significantly reduce test time and shorten the overall life cycle or time-to-market timeframe. This result coupled with inspections at each and every link in the schedule chain of tasks should make your system test almost a nonevent.

There's another interesting aspect about requirements allocation and planning that crops up when you need to do replanning. Replanning occurs when you have to repeat certain tasks based on the following:

■ Customer requirements change
■ Developmental redesigns
■ Process failures

The first item is totally out of your control and can happen anytime while executing a project schedule. The others are serious internal problems that need immediate action by engineering or the software engineering process group (SEPG). If you adopt this process model, you should never see the developmental redesigns or process problems, unless your workforce is totally inept in doing their job.

If you think about this process model, every task on your schedule is an activity instance from the process world. Every task has an object associated with that activity name. Each object is a piece/part-based object. Units are associated with a particular integration set. Integration sets are associated with a particular subsystem. Subsystems are associated with the target system. All these pieces/parts are mapped from the lowest element to the system level. All show up on your project schedule. Figure 14.9 shows those requirements allocation flows in one direction and requirements traceability in the other direction.

Now comes a customer requirements change. If we have done the requirements flow down and traceability correctly, we know what pieces/parts are affected by this change. We know what parts (or branches) of our project schedule need to be redone. This information allows us to "prune" the project schedule and move the affected schedule branches forward in the schedule, making sure we change the charge number to reflect rework. Replanning almost becomes a minor drill in identifying the affected pieces/parts as per your task (activity) objects and making that schedule section change. Rework is

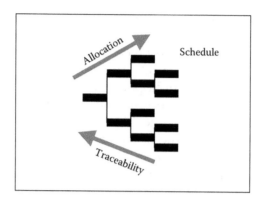

Figure 14.9 Where requirements come in for rework.

a killer for SPM. You can't avoid some rework. Others you can avoid. Just be aware that in addition to schedule pruning, you have your SPM role partners involved as well. SCM may have to reconfigure the developmental repository and project sandbox. Accounting may have to change the project's charge numbers and associated files. This process basis removes a lot of the uncertainty of exactly what is affected for a professional replanning effort, however.

To summarize project planning, the smart software project manager does the following:

- Uses activity-loaded estimates for project planning (L-AVG)
- Gets variance reporting beyond the MIN–MAX range determined from those activities
- Uses "Design Down" to determine the system piece/part story
- Gets early-up unit-based direction from engineering as a result of any "Design Down (subsystem)" task execution
- Gets unit schedule tasking direction from engineering as a result of any "Design Down (subsystem)" execution
- Insists on solid integration planning to get that unit integration set mapping and ordering
- Insists on requirements traceability down to the integration set level for schedule life cycle compaction
- Allows incremental system testing after each and every integration execution for shortened test time
- Does replanning based on requirements flow down and traceability through the process-based project schedule

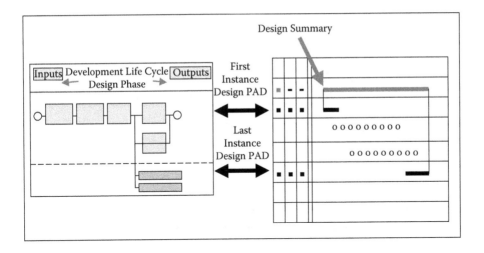

Figure 14.10   Project schedule summary determination.

One last item for planning involves project summaries. In this process model, I want to make sure that you don't confuse these two items:

- Project summary items
- Activity groups

The project summary is a phase-based (and, thus, a PAD-based) start-end rollup of pertinent activities within the PAD that shows up on a project schedule. This is shown in Figure 14.10.

The summary is derived from the beginning of the first activity instance (task) on a schedule through to the end of the last activity instance (task) on the schedule. Summaries merely show the elapsed time or durations of executing all the activities within a process-phase PAD. Summaries should not be used for progress reporting, whereas activity groups should be used for progress reporting.

From a physical schedule appearance perspective, the summary line has a name (should be noun-based) but no object or responsible person fields shown. The schedule tasks (should be verb-based) have all these fields filled in. Figure 14.11 shows this separation. The "reconcile" (or "R" column) is primarily used for tracking tasks. You could use that same field for summary line reconciliation if all the activities for that summary are done.

	Activity Names/ Summaries	Activity Objects	Activity Leads	R
Summary {	DESIGN	--	--	--
	Understand Proposal Design	Project Proposal	Jimmy Green	
Activity instances or tasks	ooo			
	ooo			
	ooo			
	Design Unit	XYZ	Susie Brown	

Figure 14.11   Summaries versus tasks on a schedule.

Chapter 15

Project Tracking

Introduction

You can't track what you didn't plan. Many traditional software project managers may have a complete schedule of what they think needs to be done based on earlier estimations. It is almost guaranteed that project estimations used to cost/price this project have no relationship to the reality of actual design/development. Woe betide that engineering lead or engineering manager who dares to tell you a story that differs from what you have in your planning schedule! I've actually seen some conflicts because of this that have come close to fistfights.

What I have described throughout this book is a project schedule with all it's tasks and predecessor/successor relationships — all based on process and actual engineering activity executions. The planning schedule used for tracking does reflect reality — not the estimation fiction. The probability of an exact alignment of planned tasks to real tasks is extremely high! Planning prior to the "Design Down (system)" is totally based on the process activity roadmaps within each phase process activity diagram (PAD). Planning after the "Design Down (system)" is based on the process activity roadmaps within each phase PAD and engineering execution of certain process activities. Tracking is based on both of these sections of the planning schedule. This relationship is shown in Figure 15.1. Engineering personnel who are the main players for design and development are also the main players for establishing the schedule built on a process foundation. This

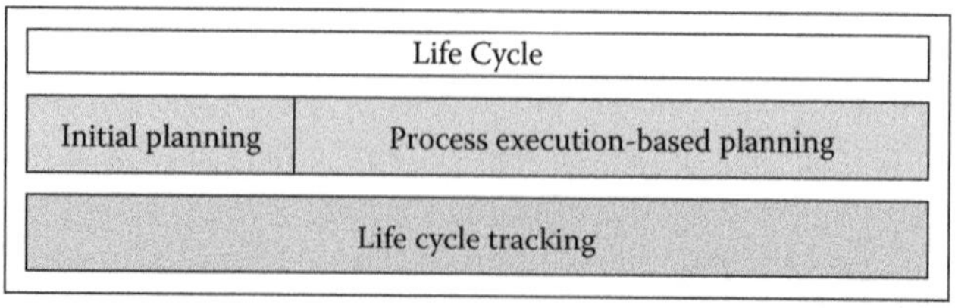

Life Cycle	
Initial planning	Process execution-based planning
Life cycle tracking	

Figure 15.1 Planning/tracking relationship.

process-based software project management (SPM) approach actually removes the software project manager to a large extent from schedule development and gives him or her more of a director role that combines process with engineering activity executions.

Using a checkbook example, you need a checkbook entry to "mark off" when reconciling a check. When an entry is not recorded, there is havoc when check reconciliation clashes with the check "plan." I want you to have a very complete and accurate portrayal of planned work to expected real work. This described process-based approach accomplishes that objective.

Planning Packages

A big difference between this approach and conventional approaches is the heart and soul of what a planning package is. Traditional planning packages (future work) have strongly suggested the need for about a six-month period for any given planning package. These planning packages have budget and statement-of-work types of information associated with them. Planning packages are also "owned" by a cost account manager. These are the entities that are converted to work packages just prior to actual work kickoff, when visibility and need dictate that conversion. Many companies (believe it or not) create planning packages from the estimations made at proposal time. These planning packages are almost guaranteed to not equal the real work to be performed because you're comparing fiction to fact. It's when reality disagrees with fiction that sparks fly between engineering and the software project manager. I've seen this a lot, and it's not pretty.

In this process-based approach, you really can't create execution-time planning packages until top-level designs are done and the software project manager has mapped out the entire schedule based on those designs. The fundamental need for traditional planning packages is questionable using this process approach because of the following:

- Schedule tasks equal activity instances.
- Schedule task estimations are the same for each activity type.
- Planning packages (if needed) comprise associated schedule tasks.

The granularity of work variance is by process activity type that is predetermined by past process activity executions. The only need for planning packages in this approach are in the following cases:

- If you organize all planning tasks by activity group and report progress metrics by each activity group (e.g., 25 percent design done)
- If you organize all planning tasks by activity object and report progress metrics for each piece/part of the system (e.g., 30 percent subsystem A done)

The former method has a granularity of cost account management (CAM) accountability down to the activity or task level, because you may never have a single cost account manager for all activities within "Design" versus "Test" etc. This method essentially makes a cost account manager out of each and every activity lead. All activity types of any given activity group become a "planning package." For example, the "Design" activity group is made up of all tasks that are "Analyze Design approaches," "Design Down," and "Design Unit" activity types. Tasks (or activity instances) on a planning schedule that are not executed are part of a planning package for that activity group. Tasks executed or being executed are equivalent to work packages for that activity group's planning package. Both are merely activity instances (or tasks) belonging to an activity group — whether executed or not. From a traditional earned value perspective, this lower granularity of CAM involvement would seem to be cumbersome. In fact, the opposite is true. Because each activity type has a predetermined set of estimates for work (duration, manpower, etc.), the activity lead (or cost account manager) has only to perform against existing engineering-based ranges established from past executions of that same activity type. That is very possible to be done.

The latter method has a higher granularity of CAM accountability for all activities related to the stated object (and its children objects). This method is used when you want a piece/part perspective of work progress. You take any and all activity types pertinent to any activity object (or its children objects) and lump them into a planning package. This method is useful when your workforce is organized by subsystems and you create planning packages by subsystem. For any given subsystem, this means taking all the tasks that directly reference that subsystem object on the schedule plus all the tasks related to the units within that subsystem, and making the subsystem lead be the cost account manager. As for the system-level activities, you can break those down by activity group within that system object (e.g., system test versus system documentation, etc.). For the system-level, it is likely that different people (and thus the cost account managers) are in charge of different aspects of that system level.

Traditional approaches to planning packages convert planning packages to work packages as work progresses. My approach does not — because both executed and unexecuted schedule tasks are all included in any given planning package by definition. Planning packages are defined at planning time after design is done and is a static entity. There is no need to go through that conversion. Because planning packages address "what needs to be done" versus any ordering of those same work elements, you don't need the integration plan information for any planning package drill. The software project manager needs the integration plan to order tasks correctly on the project schedule for maximized efficiency.

Activity Tracking

In this method, because tasks on a schedule are merely activity instances, each task completion should be tracked to a planned task on the planning schedule. Once "done," you can mark it off as done by merely placing a "✓" in the reconcile (or "R") column of your project schedule. This is shown in Figure 15.2.

This is the simplest method for tracking completed tasks versus noncompleted tasks. Because tasks equal activities, you can do all kinds of things from a metrics perspective to provide valuable progress data. I am a great believer in keeping things simple. Because all activities have predetermined static planning estimates with variances by activity type, make it easy on yourself and count "1" for each "done" task. Here are some things you could do:

■ You could add up all the tasks (activity instances) on your schedule and calculate the number done versus the total. For example, if you had 1500 tasks on your schedule and you had 300 marked with a "✓," you could report 20 percent completion for earned value.

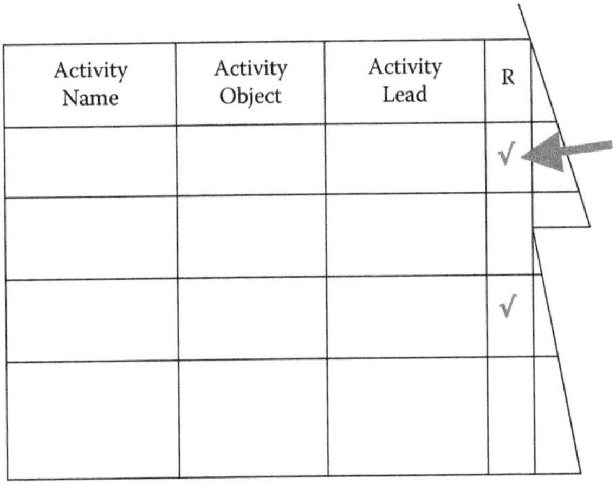

Figure 15.2 Earned value reconciliation.

■ You could take the same overall task total and break it down into activity groups. For each activity type marked with a "✓," you could take a percentage of that group and do this for all activity groups. If you had the same 1500 tasks mentioned earlier, they may break down, among others, into:
  – Requirements — 6
  – Design — 10
  – Development — 1400
  – Test — 64
  – Documentation — 20
    You might have 100 percent requirements done, 60 percent design done, 0 percent development done, 5 percent documentation done, etc.
■ You could take the major activity objects and subdivide all your tasks by that object:
  – System object — for all documentation, integration, and system testing, etc.
  – Subsystem objects — for all subsystem-related activities, including the units belonging to that subsystem
    This gives you a piece/part view of progress. For example, you could have 25 percent system work done, 80 percent subsystem A done, and 70 percent subsystem B done.

I want to revisit what "done" means for any task. Because each task is an activity, the following are predetermined:

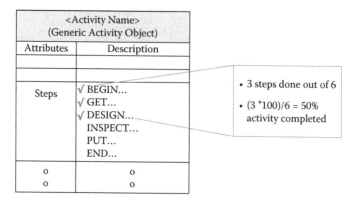

Figure 15.3 Internal activity tracking.

- Inputs
- High-level steps
- Outputs

In addition, I have predetermined that there will be certain high-level steps in all activities. The main ones for "doneness" include the following:

- BEGIN
- GET
- PUT
- INSPECT
- END

I insist on an inspection for each produced work product as part of "done." I insist on retrieving and placing your work products in a version-controlled software configuration management (SCM)-controlled repository. I insist that the END be the key driver for communicating "done" on all your schedule tasks. When an END gets executed, you can be fairly assured that you are really "done." If you have six high-level steps, each step is auditable to make sure even the most errant software task lead is indeed "done." You could even subdivide those steps if you wanted an even lower granularity of "done" within any particular activity. This is shown in Figure 15.3.

It should be obvious to the reader that because these common high-level steps exist in all activities, an inefficient "how-to" procedural connection to these common steps could have a huge detrimental ripple effect throughout the life cycle. It is for this reason that the INSPECT procedure, in particular, must be as efficient as you can make it. At one large wireless telecommunications company, I improved this particular procedure, making it six to ten times more efficient than their existing practice and improved the quality of the inspection itself as well. The practitioners dreaded the old method and loved the new one. Because of word-of-mouth advertising, other parts of the company also wanted me to train their folks on this new approach.

Similar to the activity level (although I'm well aware that each step is not weighted the same), just count the steps done versus the total steps. Make no effort to factor in step weighting — it just complicates things unnecessarily.

SCM-Based Tracking

This process approach provides yet another avenue for project tracking based on the developmental repository controlled by SCM. Traditional tracking is task based. This is work product based. I realize this may sound strange to some of you — but it is another perspective related to tracking progress.

SCM has not only set up the structure for the developmental repository based on engineering design executions but has populated that repository with version 0 files of templates and placeholders. This was done to ensure that software engineering developers could execute a GET and truly get something. It was also done to ensure the correct template for developers so that they don't have to hunt for any template. Figure 15.4 shows this SCM repository for tracking.

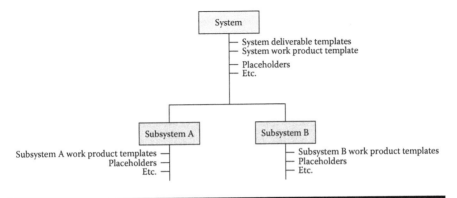

Figure 15.4   SCM developmental repository tracking.

Because of this, SCM could take a document-centric perspective and know for sure which work products are not started (i.e., still at version 0) versus those that are in progress (i.e., something other than version 0). Because of the END notification capability in this process model, it is also conceivable that SCM could capture the final versions of particular work products and make an additional call on the percentage of work products in progress versus the percentage of work products completed. This SCM perspective strictly looks at the work product picture and not the tasking picture that produced any work product. In this approach, you could easily have three task executions involved with updates on a single work product! SCM counts "1," whereas a task perspective would count "3."

Rework Tracking

Tracking is great if nothing changes between the planning schedule roadmap and the actual work being done. That is not the real world, however. The one constant in life is change. This process approach will eliminate a lot of the rework that is self-inflicted; i.e.:

- Process based
- Redesign based

What it can't do is control rework from an external source — such as requirements changes coming in from your customer (usually at the most inopportune time). When requirements change, you will invoke an event-driven procedure in this model that determines impact analysis on those changes. Requirements changes during proposal time are handled very differently from those at execution time. In this model, you would have one "how-to" at pre-execution segment time and another at execution segment time to accommodate those "how-to" differences. To determine change impact, you not only need to cost out the proposed changes on their own merit, but you need to look at where you are on the project schedule. Early requirements changes are less costly than later ones. If I had contracted a painter to paint my house blue with white trim and changed that early (before he bought the paint), the change would probably be a wash. If I decided to change the colors after he had bought the paint, I would be charged for an additional visit/labor involved in changing the order. If he had already started painting the blue and white combination when I changed my mind, the cost would include the used blue and white

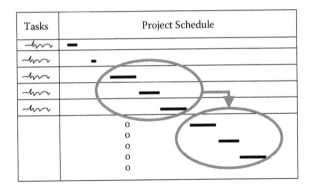

Tasks	Project Schedule

Figure 15.5 Rework tracking.

paint plus the reworked labor on the house itself. This is similar to what happens in software development. Changes prior to design are one thing. Changes at test time are enormous. These need to be factored into the change analysis.

Having said all that, the project schedule itself becomes a changed work product for the software project manager related to rework. The software project manager has to physically move whole chunks of the schedule over to be reworked. In addition, the charge numbers need to reflect a reworked task by changing the rework counter from 0 to 1. Note that if you are reworking rework, the number goes from 1 through 9 and then back to 1. If you're in that mode, you're in deep trouble. Figure 15.5 shows this rework phenomenon.

Chapter 16

Project Closedown

Introduction

There are a host of tasks you want to perform at the close of a project. Some are applicable to any project. Some have direct relevance to this process-based approach to software project management (SPM). The one act you don't want to do is delete everything and wipe the slate clean for these reasons:

- Software does not end with software development. Once in the field, you embark on the whole maintenance and support cycle. This means fixing field-related problems, updating the software, rebuilding, and rereleasing.
- Your customer may come back to you with a new order that is mostly this product with new contractual changes to be made.
- A brand new customer may want a software product that you can leverage from this product.

You can't do any of these without the development base.
So let's take a look at what you need to do at project closedown:

- You need an orderly wrap-up of the developmental repository, making sure that final delivered versions are either well understood and documented or are physically moved from software configuration management (SCM) control to a CM-controlled product release repository.

- You need to physically capture the versions of software that created this project. These include various tools, compilers, test kits, etc. The point here is that you need the entire set of stuff that can recreate that software.
- You probably need your releases in the product repository — beyond the project level. A release includes source, object, executables, version descriptions, release notes, etc. Some companies have an enterprise CM-controlled repository for these kinds of things. Control is passed from a software CM organization to a product CM organization.
- You need to either delete or archive your project sandbox. This is the working area used by all your tasks while developing your software.
- You need to collect project metrics for process improvements and to update activity-based estimations for future projects.
- You need to close down your project charge number.
- You need to close down your project resources (human and material).
- You need a postmortem that takes a look back at what went right and what went wrong so that these findings can be analyzed and handled. These findings could point to software process improvements, organizational issues to be fixed, institutional issues to be fixed, etc.

Repositories on Closedown

From an SCM perspective, we have two repositories associated with your project:

- The developmental repository. This is a version-controlled repository containing all versions of all work products produced during the course of the project's life cycle.
- The project sandbox. This is the working area for all the task executions in your project that created the work products in the developmental repository.

The former repository should not contain any version 0 file for any work product unless there's a really good reason for it. All files should have moved off that base. It is this repository that can provide a possible reconstruction of your project from a target perspective. The developmental software suite (such as compilers, linkers, loaders, tools, etc.) is another story and also needs to be captured to complete that reconstruction effort — if you need it. This repository needs to be archived in its totality. This archiving action may get into ISO 9001 issues on "how long to archive" type of questions? That's another topic, however. There is also a need to tighten controls to disallow further updates from the developmental area related to released products heading for the CM-controlled environment.

The latter repository needs to either be deleted totally or maintained as a structure only (i.e., depopulate all the sandbox areas). This repository would have some marginal value if you had to crank up the project again and didn't want to start from ground zero.

The one repository that gets built up at this stage is the product CM repository. This area should be tightly controlled. You simply cannot allow the developers to modify these CM-controlled products. CM also needs to physically capture and document all the developmental software (along with their versions), so that product releases can be reconstructed, if necessary. The product release staple is the executable module sent to the customer. The enterprise sure needs to be able to reconstruct this executable module as well.

For all this action, you need off-site backup facilities to address catastrophes, whether natural or man-made. This is true of all your intellectual properties, including the project repositories and product repository.

Metrics Collection on Closedown

This is where this process-based approach to SCM makes its mark. Because schedule tasks are the same as process activities, you can readily get real insight into your project. These are what you can do:

- Count the number of tasks for this project.
- Break that number down by activity type.
- Break that number down to activity groups.
- Get the number and type of activities by activity object.
- Get actual costs per activity type. This provides new feedback for adjusting activity-type estimations for future projects.
- Get costs per activity group.
- Get costs per system piece/part across all activities.
- Get rework costs for this project.
- Get rework costs by activity type.
- Get rework costs by activity group.

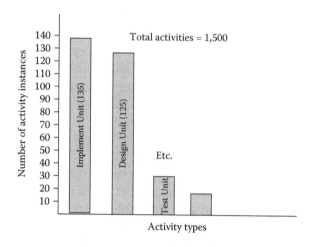

Figure 16.1   Activity story in a Pareto chart.

You may be able to think up more that you can get from this process-based approach to SPM.

You can readily see the activity (task) story for your project by taking each activity type, enumerating the activities in each type, and arranging these in a Pareto chart. Figure 16.1 shows this possibility.

This provides a really good insight into where your money was spent. It also provides your software engineering process group (SEPG) with guidance on which activity types would yield the most project execution improvement with activity process improvements.

From an enterprise perspective, a project perspective, and an organizational perspective (if you have subsystem leads), having a piece/part view is also important. Because each schedule task has an object associated with it and the object aligns with the generic object specified at the process activity, you can readily achieve this metric. This is how you do this:

- You separate all the activities at the system level from all others.
- For system objects, further separate these into the following:
  - System deliverables.
  - System analysis.
  - System test.
- For all others, separate all the subsystem A activities (including units) from subsystem B's set, and so on. Figure 16.2 might show that kind of story for subsystem A.

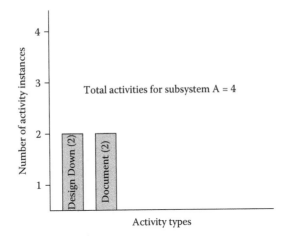

Figure 16.2 Activities by object chart.

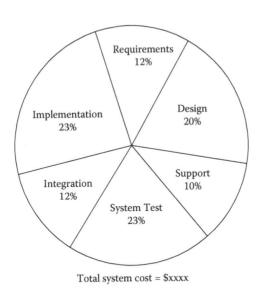

Total system cost = $xxxx

Figure 16.3 Costs by activity group pie chart.

A pie graph is a great way of seeing where your money went by activity group across your whole project. You could, for example, take percentages of the pie for each group and compare them to industry standards. Figure 16.3 shows that kind of representation.

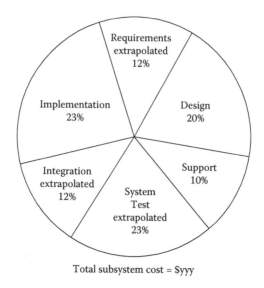

Total subsystem cost = $yyy

Figure 16.4   Cost by a subsystem piece/part.

You can do something similar for any subsystem. One possible complication could come in when you need to extrapolate costs to that subsystem. Figure 16.4 shows that kind of pie graph.

This provides not only the piece/part cost but also how that cost was distributed. Again, this is a marvelous metric.

Rework is something that you really want to control. Rework needs to be either eliminated or reduced for any company to survive. This process approach allows you a direct way to calculate rework. As a reminder, the last digit of any charge number is either 0 for original (nonreworked effort) or 1 to 9 for rework efforts. Because charge numbers are associated with schedule tasks and tasks equal process activities, we can easily determine the following:

- Percentage rework related to total cost
- Rework of rework
- Rework by activity type
- Rework by activity object
- Rework by activity group

What we can't deduce from the rework counter in the charge number is whether the rework is self-induced (process/engineering/institutional issues) or customer-caused (target requirements changes/contract changes).

Post Mortem on Closedown

I have used two of the 7M-toolsets (modified somewhat) very success-fully for a variety of purposes:

- To dig out enterprise process pain issues
- To dig out project pain issues while the project is in progress
- For preaudits and preappraisals
- For a project post mortem

These two 7M-tool techniques have fancy names:

- Infinity brainstorming
- Interrelational digraphs

I don't use these terms when I conduct these techniques; I just call them *focus groups, action groups*, or *postmortem*. Using fancy terms will turn people off. Don't do it. This particular technique is fast (less than 2 hr mostly) and is totally anonymous (no retribution). This particular technique levels the playing field for quiet introverted people versus loud dominant ones. That quiet and shy person may be the very person with a lot to express anonymously.

The most successful group session was done with about 35 people in about an hour and a half. At this point, you're probably thinking I'm crazy when I have a successful session with 35 people. Conventional wisdom says the success of any meeting is conversely proportional to the number of attendees. The higher the number of people, the lower the level of success; the lower the number of people, the higher the success level. This technique is just the opposite. You need at least 12 people to be successful. A really small group simply won't work for this technique.

Here are the supplies needed to conduct these sessions:

- Large Post-It notes — about 20 Post-Its (minimum) per participant.
- Butcher paper or flip-chart paper. These are taped to three walls of the conference room. Four or five charts are taped to one wall. Five or six charts are taped to the opposite wall. One chart is taped on a third wall (for infinity brainstorming rules). One chart will be used to capture the major impact analysis after we collect the data from the infinity brainstorming part of this session. The size of the room will determine how many

walls are actually used. No matter what, you need at least two walls for charts.

■ Masking tape for the large paper sheets already mentioned.
■ Fine-point felt pens — enough for participants and facilitator.

You need a large conference room that will hold all the participants and has wall space onto which you can tape large paper charts on three walls.

You need to reserve the room for about 2½ to 3 hr to allow for facilitator setup time, time for the actual session, and time for winding up. The participants will show up about ½ hr after the room-reserved start time. You should have all the supplies out and the charts up around the room.

This is what you need to do ahead of time:

■ Write down the session rules on a single chart. The rules are as follows:
  – One finding per Post-It.
  – You can write as many Post-Its as you want within the allotted time.
  – Use only the supplied fine-point felt pen for writing.
  – No handwriting — print your finding.
  – No names (i.e., anonymous).
  – Don't get personal — make it process related.
  – Be businesslike (but not crude) in your remarks on findings.
  – Make findings clear as to your intent. Can another person understand your point?
  – Be quiet when writing findings.

Here's how this technique works:

■ Take a few minutes to explain to the assembled group what you will be doing. Make sure the group knows about your expectations and desired end results. I have even put this in written form and sent it to the group ahead of time to make sure that everyone's on board with this technique. This sets the foundation (5 min maximum).
■ Announce that during this period of time, participants are to write one finding per Post-it® note on as many Post-it notes as you want — within that timeframe. Pens are supplied — don't use your own. This is a totally quiet part of this technique. After writing, participants take their individual Post-its and stick them

onto one wall's paper charts. Random placement is in order. This part actually brings to light all the project issues (as well as good aspects), as experienced/known by the participants, in a way that there is no retribution because no names are used (10 min maximum).

- Explain that we are now going to place the findings into "like" groupings by placing Post-its from one wall into Post-it groupings on another. Explain that, at this point, an attempt will be made to cluster similar items together and that we may have to make some adjustments later. Also point out that we have two predetermined categories called *Orphans* and *Good.* The Orphans mailbox category catches all the miscellaneous findings that we don't know where they go. The Good mailbox category is for the things we did right on a project.
- Have everyone stand up, grab a pile of Post-its from one wall, and place on another wall as Post-it clusters. Remember, one ground rule is that once a finding is established, it can't be removed. Some talk among people can happen at this point. If you do this correctly, you will try to limit the category clusters to about 10–12 groups at a maximum (about 10–12 min).
- Identify a "reader" from the group; this individual will be reading the Post-its to the entire group and possibly rearranging some Post-its (about 1–2 min).
- Have the reader stand up and read each Post-it finding aloud to the group in each cluster. This accomplishes the following:
  - Everyone gets to hear all the findings.
  - Everyone gets to persuade the reader to remove a Post-it seen as not being a good fit in that group.
  - Finally, the group establishes a mailbox name for that cluster of Post-its. Keep the name short, if possible. I found that using the names from one project as predetermined names for subsequent postmortems was helpful for metrics data. I had one group that disagreed with this and felt it was stifling to have a set of mostly predetermined names, especially when they disagreed with an earlier group over those names.
- The reader repeats this for all Post-it clusters until all cluster groups have a category name. It is during this timeframe that some Post-it notes may be moved from one group to another. Finally, an attempt is made to place any and all "orphaned" Post-it notes into a named category. If not, they stay as orphans. This part takes the findings and attempts to categorize them for the interrelational digraph part of this technique (15–20 min).

- The moderator takes a large blank matrix and writes all the category names down the left side of the matrix and then writes the same set across the top of the matrix. The moderator shades out the box in which each category intersects itself. You should end up with a diagonal line of shaded boxes from the top-left down to the bottom-right in the matrix. This is the foundation for the interrelationship digraph. We want to end up with some idea of what we need to work on first, second, third, etc., to get the biggest bang for the buck in the process (about 2 min).
- The moderator takes each category name down the left side of the matrix and asks, "What are the other categories that have a major impact on this category?" The group participates in identifying other categories that have a major impact. The moderator simply places an X across the row for the targeted category. This gets repeated for each category name down the left until the last category (10 min maximum).
- The moderator simply totals up the number of X marks per column and writes the total at the bottom of each column. This provides a really good idea of what categories should be attacked first that has the most impact on other categories (about 2 min).
- Thank the group for their time and dismiss them.

Is this a perfect technique? No. Is it fast? Yes. Does it get at postmortem issues? You bet. By spending about 1½ hr on this, you will extract both project issues as well as its good aspects from everybody. There is no retribution, because there are no names involved. The quiet person can write down stuff anonymously just as the extrovert can. The inputs come from the very people who have worked the project from the trenches.

After a session, I record all the findings by category into a Microsoft Excel spreadsheet. This is a great application to count things and to come up with percentages, etc. The completed spreadsheet gets sent back to all the participants immediately. I have cautioned this group to keep the information under wraps because it is confidential company data. This is also a good time to perform one pass through the findings and attach a role to that finding. I have found that a postmortem category can have process-related findings for the SEPG and organizational and enterprise findings for management. It is good to make this separation by role; i.e., who might be the appropriate folks to deal with a finding. The top three categories do provide some insight into what should be done first, second, third, etc.

If you use common categories across projects, it certainly opens the door to collecting some cross-project metrics related to categorized findings.

The beauty of doing a postmortem at project closedown time is that issues are still fresh with the project participants. This particular method tends to extract a lot of data so that you can constantly improve your future projects. With anonymity built-in, people are not hesitant to raise valid issues for the betterment of the entire enterprise. All in all, postmortems are well worth doing.

Hopefully, I have left you with many points to think about. Go forth and do good things.

INDEX

Index